REDEFINING YOU

The 4-step process to find **CONFIDENCE,**
CLARITY and **PURPOSE** as a woman

AMANDA CAHILL

DOWNLOAD YOUR FREE BONUS GIFT!

READ THIS FIRST

As a thank you for buying my book, I'm giving you a bonus gift to help you find confidence, clarity and purpose in your life, 100% FREE!

TO DOWNLOAD SCAN THE QR CODE:

www.amandacahill.com/redefiningyouresources

Table of Contents

Foreword

I've had the honor of knowing Amanda Cahill for several years now, and in that time, I've witnessed her remarkable transformation. Amanda is the kind of person who doesn't just talk about change—she lives it. Watching her take the tools she's learned and apply them with relentless dedication to redefine her life has been nothing short of inspiring.

When I first met Amanda, she was at a crossroads, searching for clarity and a deeper sense of purpose. Through our work together, I saw her make brave, intentional decisions to face her fears, rewrite her narrative, and step into her power. Her journey was not easy—transformations rarely are—but she showed up for herself every single day. She embraced the discomfort of growth, leaned into the process, and emerged as a stronger, more confident version of herself.

What stands out most about Amanda is her ability to take what she's learned and turn it into action. She didn't just absorb ideas or theories—she implemented them in her daily life, creating systems and habits that helped her regain her spark and build a life she loves. Now, she's sharing those same tools with you in *Redefining You*.

This book is more than a guide; it's an invitation. Amanda invites you to recognize your own strength, to take ownership of your life, and to create a future that aligns with the woman you're meant to be. Her four-step framework is practical, approachable, and deeply empowering. It's designed for the woman who's ready to stop waiting for the "right time" and start taking intentional steps toward her dreams—because Amanda knows firsthand that waiting doesn't lead to change, action does.

What I admire most about Amanda's journey—and what you'll see reflected in these pages—is her deep belief that transformation is possible for anyone who's willing to do the work. Whether you're struggling to find clarity, build confidence, or create habits that stick, Amanda's words will resonate with you. Her story is proof that no matter where you're starting from, you have the power to redefine yourself and create a life that feels authentic and fulfilling.

I couldn't be more proud of Amanda and the wisdom she's sharing here. *Redefining You* is a book that will meet you where you are and guide you to where you want to go. All you need is the courage to take the first step.

Let this be your turning point.

Sarah Centrella
Best-selling author of #Futureboards and Hustle Believe Receive

Introduction

Have you ever felt a quiet but persistent voice inside, urging you to grow, to change, to become more aligned with the woman you know you're capable of being? For years, I ignored that voice. I told myself I didn't have the time, the confidence, or the clarity to pursue the life I truly wanted. Like many women, I let fear and doubt hold me back—fear of failure, fear of judgment, and most of all, fear of stepping out of the comfortable, familiar routines that defined my life.

It wasn't until I faced a moment of deep frustration—a moment when I realized the life I was living wasn't reflective of my true self—that I began the journey of redefining myself. That journey wasn't linear or simple, but it was transformative. And that transformation is what I want for you, too.

This book is for the woman who feels stuck, who knows she's capable of more but isn't sure where to start. It's for the woman who has big dreams but feels weighed down by the day-to-day demands of life. It's for the woman who's ready to stop waiting for the "right time" and start creating the life she envisions. This book isn't about offering a one-size-fits-all roadmap to success; it's about giving you the tools, mindset, and confidence to redefine yourself on your own terms.

My Story—and Why This Matters to You

For as long as I can remember, I believed I could achieve anything I set my mind to. That belief wasn't an accident—it was a gift from my mother, a strong, independent, successful woman who taught me that if I wanted something, it was within my reach. She modeled resilience and ambition, instilling in me a sense of determination that became the foundation of my success. Watching her navigate life with confidence shaped everything I did as I grew up. But it also came with a silent, unyielding pressure: if success was possible, then failure wasn't an option. And if failure wasn't an option, then I had to be perfect.

That drive for perfection infiltrated every corner of my life—college, grad school, my career, my relationships, and eventually, motherhood. It was my constant companion, pushing me to achieve and excel but also demanding that I maintain an illusion of control and accomplishment at all times. On the outside, it looked like I had it all together. I was thriving in sales, climbing the ladder in my career, and achieving the goals I set for myself. But beneath the surface, the pressure to be perfect was suffocating. Every success felt hollow as if it was never enough. I was chasing an ideal that always seemed just out of reach.

Then came motherhood—a role I had always imagined would come naturally to me. After all, I had thrived in so many other areas of my life. Why would this be any different? But motherhood wasn't what I expected. The sleepless nights, the relentless self-doubt, the overwhelming responsibility—it all hit me harder than I could have imagined. Suddenly, I wasn't just struggling to live up to my own impossible standards. I felt like I was failing at everything.

Day by day, the spark that had always fueled me began to dim. I stopped recognizing the woman staring back at me in the mirror. One day, I looked at some pictures of myself and couldn't ignore the truth any longer: the smile was gone. The light in my eyes was missing. I saw a shell of the woman I used to be. That realization was hard to swallow. I didn't know who I was anymore, and I didn't know how to get her back.

Around that same time, I received my first-ever poor performance review at work. I can still remember how it felt, like a punch in the gut. For someone who had always defined herself by her achievements, this was a wake-up call. Everything in my life felt like it was unraveling. At home, I felt like I was falling short as a mom. At work, I was no longer excelling. Inside, I was exhausted, overwhelmed, and questioning everything. I was at rock bottom. And I was asking myself the same question you might be asking yourself right now: Is this my life? Is this all there is?

That moment could have been the end of my story. It could have been the moment I gave up, resigned to the idea that this was just how things were now. But instead, it became the beginning of something entirely new. Because in that moment of despair, I made a decision. I decided that if I wanted my life to change, I had to change. If I wanted to reclaim the woman I had been—and become the woman I envisioned—I had to start taking action.

It wasn't glamorous or easy. I didn't wake up the next morning with all the answers. But I started where I was, with what I could control. I began building small, intentional habits that aligned with the vision I had for my life. I created systems and routines that gave me space to focus on my growth and rediscover the woman I wanted to be. And I learned to let go of the perfectionism that had held me back for so long, embracing progress instead.

The results? They were beyond anything I could have imagined. Within a year of deciding to change my life, I launched a podcast called *Redefining Motherhood* (now *Redefining You*), signed a book deal to bring this very book to life, and got into the best shape of my life—yes, even after having a baby! I took on an exciting executive-level role at a new company and, most importantly, redefined who I was as a woman and as a mother. I went from surviving to thriving. From believing in my potential to becoming the woman I had always known I could be.

But here's the thing: none of this happened because I magically "figured it out." It happened because I made a choice. I chose to align my goals, habits, and intentions with the vision I had for my life. I chose to prioritize progress over perfection, showing up for myself one step at a time. And I chose to believe that even at rock bottom, there was a way forward.

That's why I'm sharing my story with you—not because I have all the answers, but because I know what it feels like to question everything. To wonder if you're capable of becoming the woman you've always envisioned. To feel stuck, overwhelmed, or invisible in your own life.

If that's where you are right now, I want you to know this: you are not alone. And it doesn't have to stay this way. You have the power to redefine yourself, to create a life that feels authentic and fulfilling. You already have everything you need within you to take the first step. It's not about being perfect. It's about progress. It's about showing up for yourself, even when it's hard. It's about believing that the woman you want to be isn't out of reach—she's already within you, waiting to be uncovered.

This book is my way of showing you how I did it and how you can do it too. It's about building confidence, creating a vision, and aligning your life with the woman you want to become. It's about taking small, intentional steps that add up to something extraordinary.

This isn't just my story. It's yours too. And I can't wait to see the woman you're about to become.

The Four-Step Framework to Redefining You

One of the biggest barriers to transformation is overwhelm. When you think about redefining yourself, it's easy to feel paralyzed by the sheer scope of what that might entail. That's why this book is structured around a simple yet powerful four-step framework, designed to help you move through the process of transformation with clarity and intention:

1. **Build Confidence:** Before you can redefine yourself, you have to believe it's possible. Confidence isn't about knowing you'll succeed—it's about trusting yourself enough to take the first step, even when the path ahead is uncertain. This step will help

you silence self-doubt, overcome fear, and develop a foundation of self-trust.

2. **Create Your Vision:** Transformation requires direction. Without a clear vision, it's easy to feel lost or aimless. This step will guide you in crafting a vision that's deeply aligned with your values, dreams, and unique identity. Your vision becomes your North Star, guiding your decisions and inspiring your actions.

3. **Cultivate Disciplined Habits:** Big changes happen through small, consistent actions. This step will help you identify the goals and habits that support your vision and show you how to build momentum through disciplined, intentional effort. You'll learn how to turn goals into daily practices that create lasting transformation.

4. **Embrace Progress Over Perfection:** The fear of imperfection is one of the biggest obstacles to growth. This step will teach you how to celebrate small wins, learn from setbacks, and keep moving forward—even when the journey feels messy. Progress, not perfection, is the true measure of transformation.

Each of these steps is designed to address a specific challenge that women face when they're trying to redefine themselves. Together, they create a roadmap that's both practical and empowering.

A Glimpse of What's Possible

To help you understand the power of this framework, let me share a glimpse of what it can look like in action. When I first decided to start a podcast, I was terrified. I had no idea where to begin, and the fear of imperfection nearly stopped me in my tracks. But I took a deep breath and embraced progress over perfection. My first episode wasn't polished or perfect, but it was a start. Over time, that podcast grew into something bigger than I ever imagined, reaching women in over 50 countries and creating a ripple effect of inspiration.

The same principles that helped me launch that podcast—confidence, vision, habits, and progress—are the principles that will guide you as you redefine yourself. Whether your dream is to start a business, improve your health, strengthen your relationships, or simply feel more aligned with your true self, this framework will help you move forward with intention and courage.

Your Journey, Your Rules

This book is not about prescribing a specific path for you to follow. It's about giving you the tools and insights to create your own path. Your journey will look different from mine, and that's exactly how it should be. You are the expert on your life, and you have the power to define what success, fulfillment, and happiness look like for you.

Throughout these pages, you'll find personal stories, practical exercises, and thought-provoking questions to help you reflect on your journey and take meaningful action. You'll be encouraged to think deeply, act intentionally, and celebrate your progress along the way.

An Invitation to Begin

As you turn these pages, I want you to remember one thing: You are already enough. This journey isn't about becoming someone else; it's about becoming the truest, most aligned version of yourself. You have everything you need within you to create the life you've always envisioned—you just need the tools to unlock it.

So take a deep breath, and let's begin. This is your time to step into your power, redefine yourself, and create a life that feels deeply, authentically yours.

How to Get the Most out of This Book

To truly redefine the woman you are and embrace the life you've always wanted, this journey begins with you taking ownership. You hold the power to create meaningful change, but it all starts with acknowledging that you have a say in how your life unfolds. Every choice you make, every step you take, moves you closer to the woman you're meant to become. You are not a bystander in your own life—you are the author, and with every chapter, you have the ability to write a new narrative.

Most people want to jump straight to the habits they need to form (for example, what time do I need to wake up to be successful?), but you need to go through self-discovery BEFORE you determine what those habits are. A lot of your problems arise from trying to form habits in your life that somebody else created for you. And where has that gotten you up to this point?

This book is more than just a collection of thoughts or ideas. It's a guide, a tool, and a mirror. It will reflect back to you what is possible when you decide to step into your power and take control of your own story. To get the most out of this book, I invite you to be open, curious, and, most importantly, committed. Real change happens when you lean in, take action, and start believing in your ability to shape your own destiny.

Throughout this book, I'll ask you to reflect, envision, and define who you are and who you want to become. My goal isn't to add more to your plate, but more to streamline your success and transformation so that your life feels more at ease, has more purpose, and you feel more intentional in your own life. But remember, none of this will stick unless you take ownership of your growth. You can't passively read and expect to see results. You've got to show up for yourself, and when you do, you'll see just how much power you truly hold.

Managing Expectations

Redefining who you are, changing your mindset, and building new habits takes time. This book is designed to help you do the deep work, but that means it's going to require effort on your part. There will be moments where it feels challenging, where you might doubt whether you're making progress. And that's okay. Real, lasting transformation doesn't happen in a straight line, and it certainly doesn't happen without a little discomfort.

Each section in this book is designed to move you forward in your journey, but it's important to go at your own pace. There's no rush— this is your life we're talking about, and meaningful change takes time. You might need to sit with certain sections longer than others, and that's perfectly fine. Progress is progress, no matter how slow it may feel.

I encourage you to manage your expectations from the start. This book will guide you, support you, and give you the tools to create the woman you want to become. But it will also ask you to do the work. And I promise you, it's worth it. Every bit of effort you invest in yourself will pay off in ways you can't even imagine right now. Be patient, be kind to yourself, and trust that the process is working, even when it feels slow.

At the end of the day, this journey is about becoming the best version of yourself, and that's something worth putting in the time for. You're building a foundation that will carry you through life—not just for today, but for years to come. So, take a breath, embrace the work ahead, and know that you've got everything it takes to become the woman you've always known you could be.

Are you ready? Let's get started!

SECTION 1:
CONFIDENCE FOUNDATION

CHAPTER 1

Redefine Your Confidence

"The most alluring thing a woman can have is confidence." – Beyoncé

Confidence isn't something we're born with; it's a skill that grows and evolves through intentional effort. This chapter explores the journey of building belief in yourself and how confidence acts as a foundational quality that empowers every other area of life.

My journey toward confidence began during one of the most challenging seasons of my life: postpartum. Six months into motherhood, I felt like I was losing my identity, my confidence, and my sense of self. It was as if the light inside me had dimmed, and I could barely recognize myself. The moments I spent doubting myself as a mother, wife, and professional were overwhelming, but they were also the beginning of my realization that confidence isn't an inherent trait—it's a practice, a skill, and a commitment to self-belief.

I vividly remember one afternoon, sitting on the edge of the bed, tears streaming down my face, while my husband sat beside me, trying to comfort me. I told him that I felt like I was failing in every aspect of my life. The woman I once was—strong, confident, and full of life—felt like a distant memory. I told my husband I wanted to give up on everything. Thankfully, I never contemplated ending my life, but I did want to crawl into a hole and never come out—I just wanted all the pain and sadness to stop. Will I ever be happy again? Will I ever know myself again? In that vulnerable moment, my husband reminded me of all the things I had accomplished, the resilience I'd shown, and the love and dedication I brought to our family. He told me how much he loved me and how it scared him to see me in this state. He knew I wasn't okay, but he didn't know how to help.

What stands out most about that time was how dark and isolating it felt. On some days, I couldn't muster the strength to believe that things could get better. But over the course of many conversations, my husband's words slowly began to crack the wall of doubt I had built around myself. I began to wonder: What if he's right? What if I could find my way back to feeling like myself again—not the old version of me, but a stronger, more aligned version?

We continued to talk through what I was going through over several weeks. During that time, my husband continued to find ways to highlight how great I was at being a mom and how proud he was to see me navigate motherhood with such ease and an innate ability to care for our son. He told me I was worthy and that I was enough just as I was. He reminded me of all the things I had accomplished before this season, and how much success I'd had along the way. He mentioned friendships that I'd cultivated, a thriving career, and how my ambition has brought some truly remarkable people and experiences into our lives. From time to time, he would even ask me to think back to moments that brought me happiness and made me proud. The more he began to find ways to bring up all that I had accomplished up to this point, the more I believed I would make it through this challenging season. In reflection, I realized what he was doing in that moment was building up my confidence when I didn't have any. He helped me realize all the beautiful moments that have created this wonderful life we live together.

Now that I'm on the other side of that hardship, I can see so clearly how important confidence is to build and maintain throughout the journey of life. His words, spoken with love and conviction, helped me start to rebuild my belief in myself. I began to realize that nobody was coming to save me, and the next step in my life would be an inside job. If I wanted to live a life full and happy again, I needed to find a way to build and reclaim my confidence.

The Challenge of Building Confidence in New Seasons of Life

Confidence is often seen as an innate quality, but in reality, it's more like a muscle that needs regular exercise. Just as our physical muscles grow stronger through resistance, confidence is strengthened when we push through moments of self-doubt and step outside of our comfort zones.

At its core, confidence is the belief in your own worth and abilities. It's the quiet assurance that you are enough, just as you are. Confidence doesn't mean you won't feel fear or doubt; it means trusting yourself to navigate those feelings. Building and maintaining confidence can be especially challenging when you're juggling multiple roles and responsibilities.

For me, motherhood brought this challenge to the forefront. Suddenly, I was not only balancing a demanding career but also the expectations and pressures of being a mom. Even if you're not a mom, I bet you know firsthand the stress that builds and how your confidence can waver when the demands of life pile high. It's in those moments—when you're stretched thin and feel like you have nothing left to give—that building confidence becomes a lifeline. The truth I've come to realize is this: Confidence isn't a destination; it's a journey that requires daily intention and action.

Common Obstacles to Confidence

There are countless obstacles that can erode our confidence, especially as we take on new roles and responsibilities. Here are some of the most common barriers:

Comparison

In a world saturated with social media and curated images of perfection, it's easy to fall into the trap of comparison. We compare our behind-the-scenes with someone else's highlight reel and wonder why we don't measure up. Confidence quickly falters when we start viewing ourselves through the lens of someone else's life.

Comparison can be particularly challenging when you're in a vulnerable season of life. I remember scrolling through Instagram during those early postpartum months and feeling like every other mom had it all figured out. Their homes were spotless, their babies were always smiling, and they looked radiant. Meanwhile, I was struggling to make it through the day, my hair in a messy bun, I hadn't showered in a few days, and I couldn't tell you the last time I slept longer than a two- to three-hour stretch at a time. I couldn't help but wonder: *What am I doing wrong? Why can't I be like them?*

What I didn't see in those perfectly polished photos were the struggles behind the scenes. The sleepless nights, the moments of doubt, and the messiness that comes with life. Over time, I began to remind myself that social media shows a highlight reel, not the full story. I also learned to put boundaries around my social media use. I started following accounts that focused on authenticity rather than perfection and unfollowed accounts that triggered feelings of inadequacy, which made a world of difference.

A helpful strategy I've used—and one I encourage you to try—is a social media cleanse. For one week, commit to only engaging with accounts that uplift and inspire you. Pay attention to how you feel after scrolling. If you notice accounts that spark negativity or self-doubt, unfollow or mute them. Protecting your mental space isn't selfish—it's a powerful act of self-care.

The truth is, no two journeys are the same. Comparison only takes away from the beauty of your own story. Instead of measuring yourself against others, try focusing on your unique path and celebrating the steps you've taken along the way.

Societal Pressure

Society often places impossible expectations on women—to excel in their careers, maintain a perfect personal life, support everyone around them, and make it all look effortless. These pressures are amplified in professional settings, where societal norms clash with personal ambition, leaving many women questioning their worth and choices.

Before I became a mother, I vividly recall how these expectations shaped my experience as a woman navigating a male-dominated industry. At the time, I was thriving in my career, taking on leadership roles and earning recognition for my contributions. Yet, there was one question that followed me everywhere: "When are you going to start a family?" It was almost always followed by unsolicited advice. "You'll have to slow down," someone would say. "You won't want to keep working at this level when you have kids." Others would casually suggest, "Let your husband take care of you. Why push so hard?"

While these comments often came with a smile, they carried an underlying assumption that my career aspirations would—and should—take a back seat to traditional expectations of motherhood and family life. At first, I laughed them off, confident in my ability to define my own path. But over time, the constant remarks began to chip away at my sense of self. I started questioning whether I could truly have it all: a fulfilling career and a personal life on my terms. Was I selfish for wanting to succeed professionally? Would I be judged if I chose a different path than the one expected of me?

This pressure reached a breaking point one evening after a networking event, where a senior colleague had told me, "You're doing so well now, but you'll have to step back eventually. That's just how it works." I went home that night feeling small, as if my hard work and achievements were irrelevant in the face of societal expectations. It was a painful reminder of how easily external opinions can make us question our choices and self-worth.

But here's what I learned: societal pressure only has power if we allow it to dictate our decisions. That moment became a turning point for me. I realized I had been letting the expectations of others take up too much space in my life. Why was I allowing someone else's vision of success to define my worth? Why was I questioning my ability to build the life I wanted, rather than the life others assumed I should have? One of the quotes I've come to learn over the years is "Never let insignificant people make a significant impact on your life."

Letting go of societal pressure isn't easy, but it starts with reclaiming your narrative. I decided to focus on what mattered to me—my career, my ambitions, and the life I wanted to create. I learned to set boundaries, trust my instincts, and define success on my own terms. It was liberating to stop seeking validation from others and start living in alignment with my values.

This journey isn't about perfection; it's about authenticity. When you stop letting societal expectations steer your choices, you create space to build a life that feels true to you—a life that celebrates your unique path, your ambitions, and your power to choose.

Perfectionism

Perfectionism is one of the sneakiest confidence killers. Many of us set impossibly high standards for ourselves, measuring our worth against an ideal that's often unattainable—and, quite honestly, unnecessary.

Perfectionism keeps us trapped in a cycle of striving and self-criticism, making it hard to feel good enough.

One of my biggest battles with perfectionism came during the early days of motherhood. As a new mom, I felt this immense pressure to do everything "right." I obsessed over every detail—from perfectly sterilizing bottles to following every piece of advice about feeding schedules, sleep routines, and developmental milestones. I spent hours reading parenting books and Googling everything, convinced that if I just worked hard enough, I could ensure my baby was always happy, healthy, and ahead of the curve.

But the reality of caring for a newborn is anything but perfect. I remember one sleepless night when nothing I did could calm my baby. I had followed every rule, every checklist, and yet I still felt like I was failing. My baby was crying, I was crying, and all I could think was, "What am I doing wrong?" I was so consumed with trying to be the perfect mom that I couldn't see the truth: babies don't need perfection—they need love, care, and presence.

That experience taught me that chasing perfection often comes at the expense of our well-being—and it's rarely necessary. My baby didn't need a mom who had it all figured out. My baby needed a mom who was there, who showed up and loved them through the chaos, the mess, and the exhaustion.

Confidence doesn't come from being flawless; it comes from showing up, doing your best, and giving yourself grace when things don't go perfectly. Instead of striving for perfection, try striving for progress. Focus on what truly matters and remind yourself that done is often better than perfect. Letting go of perfectionism doesn't mean letting go of care or effort—it means freeing yourself to show up authentically and embrace the beauty of imperfection.

Mental Load

The mental load—the invisible labor that comes with managing a household, caring for others, and balancing a career—can be incredibly heavy. It's the never-ending to-do list that lives in your head: Prepping for a big meeting, planning date nights with your spouse, remembering doctor's appointments, keeping the house clean, planning meals, scheduling playdates, and making sure everything runs smoothly. It's easy to feel like you're always one step away from dropping the ball, which can chip away at your confidence over time.

I remember a specific day when the mental load completely overwhelmed me. I had just wrapped up a long workday filled with back-to-back meetings, and I was rushing to pick up my son from daycare. As I walked through the door, I realized I'd forgotten to pack a crucial item for his diaper bag that morning. The daycare worker gave me a kind reminder, but I felt a wave of shame. *How could I forget something so simple? Why can't I get it together?*

Later that evening, I broke down to my husband, listing all the things I had been trying to juggle and how I felt like I was failing at everything. He looked at me and said, "You're doing so much more than you give yourself credit for. You don't have to carry all of this alone." That conversation was a turning point for me. I started delegating tasks (to him, nonetheless), setting boundaries, and, most importantly, giving myself permission to ask for help.

The truth is you don't have to do it all. Delegating, saying no, and setting realistic expectations aren't signs of weakness—they're signs of strength. Lightening the mental load creates space to focus on what truly matters and helps you show up as your best, most confident self.

Belief in Yourself: The Foundation of Confidence

At the end of the day, confidence is rooted in belief—in believing that you are enough, that you are worthy, and that you are capable of achieving the life you desire. This belief isn't always easy to cultivate, especially in a world that often tries to tell us otherwise. But it's essential.

Belief in yourself is the foundation upon which confidence is built. It's what allows you to take risks, to pursue your dreams, and to stand tall in the face of adversity. It's what gives you the courage to redefine yourself, to create a life that is true to who you are and what you want.

This is where the concept of self-efficacy, introduced by psychologist Albert Bandura, becomes so important. Self-efficacy is the belief in your ability to influence events and outcomes in your life. Research has shown that people with high self-efficacy are more likely to set challenging goals, persevere through difficulties, and, ultimately, achieve success. The more you prove to yourself that you're capable—through small wins, daily actions, and reframing self-doubt—the stronger your self-belief becomes.

Think of self-belief as a garden. Each time you nurture it with positive actions, encouraging words, or small victories, you're planting seeds. Those seeds grow over time into a vibrant, flourishing garden that becomes the foundation for your confidence. Conversely, neglecting that garden—through negative self-talk or comparison—can cause it to wither. The good news? It's never too late to start planting.

As you continue on your journey of self-discovery and growth, remember this: Confidence is not a destination; it's a practice. It's something you cultivate every day in the choices you make and the way you treat yourself. Be kind to yourself. Trust yourself. And know that you are worthy of all the love, joy, and success that life has to offer.

You are more than enough, just as you are. And with each step forward, you are building a life that reflects the beautiful, powerful, and confident woman you are becoming.

Exercises for Building Confidence

These practical exercises are designed to help you cultivate self-belief and strengthen your confidence muscle. Remember, confidence is a skill, and like any skill, it improves with consistent practice. The more you do these exercises, the easier it becomes to build your confidence. It's like a snowball effect: each day builds on the next until you begin to feel unstoppable. As you go through this list of exercises for building confidence, I want to encourage you to pick one or two exercises that resonate with you the most and only focus on those to start. Often, when we find failure in trying something new, it's that we try to take on too much at one time. A great example of this is someone who has never run before going out the first day and trying to run five miles. Unless this person is superhuman, I bet they fall short and only make it one or two miles (if that!) before they call it quits. But if that same person went out the first day knowing they were only going to run one mile and gave themselves the strategy of running for 30 seconds and walking for 30 seconds until the mile was complete, I bet they would have a higher likelihood of succeeding. And the next time they went out to run, they could run for 40 seconds and walk for 20 seconds until the mile was complete and they would progress from there with each time they went to run. Start slow and progress from there. Don't try to take on everything at once.

Daily Confidence Check-In

Start each day by acknowledging one thing you're proud of or grateful for. It doesn't have to be grand—small wins add up over time and create a solid foundation for confidence. Maybe you drank water before having coffee this morning—be proud of that choice to care for your body. Did you hold your cool yesterday during a tense meeting while a coworker kept interrupting? That's a win. Perhaps you simply got out of bed on a challenging day—acknowledge the resilience it took to do that. Even the act of waking up and feeling grateful for a new day is worth celebrating.

This daily check-in is about intentionally shifting your focus to what's working, rather than dwelling on what isn't. By consistently practicing this exercise, you begin to rewire your brain to notice the positives in your day-to-day life. Over time, this builds a strong foundation of self-belief and gratitude.

For even greater impact, write down what you're proud of or grateful for in a journal or on a sticky note you can see throughout the day. Visual reminders reinforce your wins and help combat moments of self-doubt. Remember, confidence grows when you celebrate small moments of progress and remind yourself that you're worthy, capable, and resilient—every single day.

Create a "Confidence Resume"

Make a list of past achievements, both big and small. This can include professional milestones, personal victories, or times when you overcame challenges. Place this resume somewhere visible as a reminder of your strengths. More on the confidence resume in Chapter 2!

Reframe Self-Doubt

When you catch yourself thinking, *I can't do this* or *I'm not enough*, pause and challenge that thought. Ask yourself: *Is this really true?* Often, self-doubt is a reaction to fear or insecurity, not a reflection of your actual abilities. By identifying these thoughts as temporary and not absolute, you create space to shift your perspective. Replace those doubts with empowering statements like, "I am learning and growing," or "I am capable of figuring this out." This small but powerful action helps train your mind to embrace self-belief, even on the hard days.

To make this exercise even more impactful, try writing down the negative thought, crossing it out, and replacing it with a positive, affirming statement. For example, change "I'm not good enough for this role" into "I bring unique strengths to every opportunity, and I'm growing every day." The act of physically crossing out the doubt reinforces the shift in your mindset.

Reframing self-doubt is a practice, not a one-time fix. Each time you challenge those negative thoughts, you're building a stronger foundation of self-trust and resilience. Over time, you'll find that your inner dialogue shifts naturally toward self-belief and encouragement. Remember, confidence isn't about having all the answers—it's about trusting yourself to navigate the journey, step by step. We'll take a deeper dive into self-belief in Chapter 3.

Keep a Record of Wins

At the end of each week, write down three moments that made you feel proud or accomplished. Over time, these small reflections add up, creating a powerful reminder of your resilience and capabilities. Also, can you imagine how powerful it would be if, at the end of the year, you have 52 weeks of wins written down? That's 156 wins for the year if you committed to writing down three wins every week. Celebrate your victories, no matter how small they may seem. Each one is a building block of your confidence, a reminder that you are more capable and powerful than you sometimes give yourself credit for.

Keeping a record of your achievements, whether they're big or small, helps you see the progress you're making over time. It's easy to forget how far you've come, especially when you're caught up in the hustle and bustle of daily life. But by tracking your successes, you create a tangible reminder of your growth and evolution.

This is a habit I got into a few years ago, and it was one that has helped me tremendously over the past year as I redefined myself. Every day I make a point to write down three things in my day planner that were wins from the day. It could be as simple as, I made someone smile, I got in my workout like I said I would, or I was fully present with my son in the morning before daycare drop-off. At the end of the week, I make a list of my top five accomplishments or wins. At the end of the month, I have 20 wins to reflect back on and celebrate. At the end of the year, that gives me 240 wins. That's huge. Imagine how you'd feel about yourself if you kept an inventory like that.

Start by setting aside time each day, week, month, and year to reflect on your accomplishments. You can do this in a journal, a digital document, or even through voice memos—whatever method works best for you. List out the things you've achieved, the challenges you've overcome, and the steps you've taken toward your goals. Be sure to include both personal and professional wins, as both contribute to your overall confidence.

Tracking your accomplishments isn't just about looking back; it's also about setting the stage for future growth. As you review your successes, you'll begin to notice patterns in your strengths and areas where you excel. This insight can help you set new goals that align with your strengths and push you to continue growing.

Getting Comfortable with the Uncomfortable

One of the biggest challenges to building confidence is the discomfort that often comes with growth. It's so tempting to stay in our comfort zones, where things feel familiar and safe, but true confidence is forged by stepping outside of that safety net and embracing the unknown. This means allowing yourself to make mistakes, being okay with not having all the answers, and leaning into the moments where you feel out of your depth.

Think of it like a workout. The first time you try a new exercise, your muscles protest—it's uncomfortable, maybe even a little painful. But with each repetition, you build strength and endurance, and over time, that once-challenging movement becomes second nature. Confidence works the same way. Each time you stretch beyond what feels easy or familiar, you're proving to yourself that you can navigate the unfamiliar and handle whatever comes your way.

Start small. Maybe it's saying yes to an opportunity that feels slightly intimidating or speaking up in a meeting when you'd typically stay silent. These small acts of courage build over time. After each step outside your comfort zone, reflect on what you accomplished and how it made you feel. Celebrate the bravery it took to try.

Growth is inherently uncomfortable, but it's also where the magic happens. The more you embrace discomfort, the more you'll discover just how resilient, capable, and confident you truly are.

Building Confidence Through Small Actions

Confidence isn't just a feeling; it's something we cultivate through action. Each small step we take reinforces our belief in ourselves. For me, rebuilding my confidence started with the tiniest of steps—so small that they felt almost insignificant at the time. I wasn't trying to overhaul my entire life all at once; I just needed a starting point, something manageable that reminded me I had the power to create change.

One of the first actions I took was setting aside time for self-care. I had been neglecting myself for months, putting everyone else's needs before my own, but I realized that if I wanted to feel differently about myself, I had to start treating myself like someone who mattered. So, I decided to prioritize one simple thing: walking outside in the mornings. At first, it didn't feel like much. I'd throw on sneakers, step outside, and walk for 15 minutes. Some mornings, I wasn't even sure why I was doing it—I didn't feel motivated, but I went anyway. There's something about the crisp morning air and the sound of your own footsteps that quiets the noise in your mind. With each walk, I began to feel a little lighter, a little clearer. And without realizing it, I was sending myself a powerful message: *You're worth showing up for.*

Around the same time, I decided to return to my meditation practice. It wasn't anything fancy—just five minutes a day of sitting still and focusing on my breath. In those quiet moments, I wasn't solving all my problems or suddenly transforming into a confident person. But I was creating space for myself to just be, without judgment or expectation. That, too, was a small act of self-respect, and it mattered.

As I continued to show up for these small actions day after day, something began to shift. I didn't feel like a completely different person overnight, but I noticed small changes. I started to stand a little taller, speak up more often, and feel less overwhelmed by my to-do list. Those tiny steps were adding up, building a case in my mind that I was capable, resilient, and worth investing in.

One morning, during my walk, I remember thinking, *This is how change happens.* It's not about a dramatic leap or waiting for the perfect moment. It starts with a decision—a single, quiet choice to do something differently. That's when the dialogue in my head shifted. Instead of asking, "What's the point?" I began asking, "What's the next step?"

If there's one thing I've learned, it's that confidence grows through momentum. The hardest part is often just starting. But once you take that first step, no matter how small, you're proving to yourself that you have some control over your life. And that's where true confidence begins—not in the absence of fear or doubt, but in the courage to move forward anyway.

Here's the truth: we always think we have little control over our lives, but that's not true. You have more power than you realize, and every small action you take is a declaration of that power. It's how you start to bridge the gap between where you are and where you want to be. Whether it's walking, journaling, calling a friend, or setting a boundary, these small steps are the building blocks of confidence.

As you continue your own journey, remember that confidence is not about being flawless; it's about embracing the process with all its twists and turns. Some days, your actions will feel effortless. Other days, it'll take everything you have just to show up. Both are valid, and both are part of the journey. Trust yourself, celebrate your wins—no matter how small—and give yourself grace on the days when confidence feels elusive.

Every small action you take is a vote for the person you want to become. Over time, those votes add up, and you'll start to see yourself differently. You'll begin to believe in your own strength and recognize that you have the power to create meaningful change in your life. And that is something truly powerful.

Grab your journal and reflect on these questions:

- Where do you feel comparison showing up in your life?

- Where are you falling into the trap of placing unrealistic expectations on yourself?

- Do you feel pressure to be perfect in any area of your life?

- Are you taking on too much? How's your mental load?

- What small action(s) can you take this week to help build confidence?

Access the free workbook by scanning the QR code:

https://www.amandacahill.com/redefiningyouresources

Key Takeaways on Confidence

- **Confidence Is a Skill, Not a Trait**: Confidence isn't something you're born with; it's something you build through consistent practice, self-reflection, and intentional action.

- **Confidence Is Rooted in Self-Belief:** At its core, confidence comes from believing in your worth and capabilities. It's not about being fearless but about trusting yourself to navigate challenges and uncertainty.

- **The Power of Small Steps:** Building confidence doesn't require dramatic leaps. It starts with small, consistent actions that remind you of your ability to create change in your life.

- **Your Journey Shapes Your Confidence**: Confidence is often tested during life's biggest transitions. In challenging moments it's possible to rediscover and rebuild belief in yourself by reflecting on your past achievements and personal strengths.

- **Confidence Requires Action**: Confidence grows when you face challenges, take risks, and embrace progress over perfection. Small steps, repeated consistently, create momentum and strengthen self-belief.

- **Comparison Is the Enemy of Confidence**: Comparing your life to others' highlight reels diminishes your self-worth. Reframe your mindset by focusing on your unique journey and placing boundaries around comparison triggers, like social media.

- **Societal Expectations Are Not Your Standards**: Let go of the pressure to conform to societal norms and expectations. Confidence is about defining success on your own terms and living authentically.

- **Perfectionism Drains Confidence**: The pursuit of perfection often leads to burnout and dissatisfaction. Instead, prioritize progress and embrace the beauty of imperfection.

- **Mental Load Impacts Confidence**: Balancing work, family, and personal responsibilities can feel overwhelming. Delegate, ask for help, and recognize that lightening your mental load strengthens your ability to show up as your best self.

- **Celebrate Your Wins**: Every success, no matter how small, contributes to your confidence. Documenting and reflecting on your achievements builds a reservoir of self-belief to draw upon in moments of doubt.

- **Comfort Zones Don't Build Confidence:** Growth requires stepping into discomfort. Each time you push past fear or doubt, you strengthen your belief in your ability to handle the unknown.

- **Confidence Is a Journey:** Confidence isn't a fixed destination but an evolving practice. Some days will feel easier than others, but every step forward strengthens the foundation of belief in yourself.

- **You Have the Power to Create Change:** Confidence grows through action. Each small step you take is a declaration of your strength and ability to shape your life.

CHAPTER 2

Redefine Your Accomplishments

"Your accomplishments are not measured by what the world recognizes, but by what you have overcome to achieve them." – Unknown

One of the most powerful tools for building confidence is looking back on what you've already achieved. Often, we brush off our accomplishments, attributing them to luck or downplaying them as minor victories. But when we take the time to truly recognize our past successes, we start to see a pattern of resilience, strength, and capability that can be a powerful foundation for self-belief.

In this chapter, I'll guide you through the process of building a "Confidence Resume." This is not about boasting or exaggerating your achievements. It's about acknowledging and celebrating the moments that have shaped you, the challenges you've overcome, and the strengths you've developed along the way.

Why We Downplay Our Successes

Many of us are conditioned to downplay our accomplishments. Society often teaches us that humility means ignoring our wins, that confidence is somehow tied to arrogance. But true confidence isn't about believing you're better than others; it's about understanding and appreciating your unique strengths and experiences. It's about owning your story, your hard work, and the growth you've earned along the way.

Growing up, I frequently heard phrases like, "Don't brag" or "Stay humble." While those values have their place, they often overshadow the importance of acknowledging our wins. The result? We hesitate to celebrate ourselves for fear of being seen as boastful. This conditioning can be so ingrained that we dismiss our achievements as "not a big deal" or attribute them to luck. Over time, this habit not only erodes our confidence but also teaches others to overlook the value we bring.

I remember a moment early in my career that exemplifies this all too well. I had just secured a major client for my team—a client that would significantly boost our revenue for the year. I had spent weeks crafting a strategy, tailoring every pitch to their unique needs, and navigating a tense negotiation process to close the deal. When my manager praised me during a team meeting, I deflected immediately. "Oh, I just got lucky," I said, brushing off the accomplishment as though it had fallen into my lap.

After the meeting, one of my mentors pulled me aside. She looked me in the eye and said, "Amanda, stop selling yourself short. That wasn't luck—it was skill. You did the research, you built the relationship, and you closed the deal. If you don't own that, how will anyone else see it?" Her words hit me like a ton of bricks. She was right. By downplaying my effort, I wasn't just diminishing my own confidence—I was sending a message to my team that my contributions weren't significant. That moment stayed with me, and over time, I began to recognize the power of celebrating my wins, no matter how uncomfortable it felt at first.

Reflecting on your achievements isn't about dwelling on the past—it's about building a foundation of confidence that you can draw on in moments of doubt. Every experience, every success, every challenge you've overcome adds to the reservoir of self-belief that fuels your journey forward. It's not always easy to unlearn the habit of downplaying yourself. The voice in your head might still whisper, *Who are you to celebrate this?* But when that happens, pause and ask yourself: *Who am I not to?* Your accomplishments are a testament to your perseverance, your talent, and your growth. They deserve to be recognized—not just by others, but by you.

Imagine what would happen if you flipped the script. Instead of dismissing your wins, what if you celebrated them? What if, the next time someone complimented your work, you simply said, "Thank you, I worked hard on that"? That small act of acknowledgment is a step toward rewiring the narrative society has written for us. It's not arrogance—it's self-respect. By owning your achievements, you also give others permission to do the same. You become a role model, showing the people around you that it's okay to be proud of their contributions. This isn't just about you—it's about shifting the culture, one win at a time.

Confidence isn't built on one big success; it's cultivated through countless small victories, each one a reminder of your capability and strength. When you take the time to reflect on your journey, to see your wins for what they truly are, you create a foundation of self-belief that no one can take away. So, the next time you catch yourself brushing off a compliment or downplaying an accomplishment, pause. Replace the dismissive thought with a celebratory one. You've earned it.

The Power of a Confidence Resume

When I was navigating the postpartum period, I felt like my confidence was at an all-time low. I remember sitting at my desk, staring blankly at my computer screen, trying to summon the courage to take on a new project at work. The opportunity was exciting, but all I could think about was how unqualified I felt. *What if I mess this up? What if they realize I'm not as capable as they think I am?* Those questions swirled in my mind, paralyzing me. That's when I pulled out my Confidence Resume—a list I had started years earlier but had almost forgotten about.

This was no ordinary resume. It wasn't about job titles or responsibilities. My Confidence Resume was a list of all the accomplishments, big and small, that I could be proud of. I first learned about this idea from my former Bold Women Society business partner, Caytie Langford, and it completely shifted the way I thought about celebrating my wins. My list included career milestones, personal achievements, and even moments of joy or resilience that had shaped who I was.

As I read through the milestones and moments I'd documented—from earning my master's degree in record time to running half marathons—I felt a spark of reassurance. These were tangible reminders of my strength, resilience, and ability to persevere. I could feel the tension in my shoulders begin to ease. That list didn't just boost my confidence—it reminded me of who I was at my core, and that was exactly what I needed to move forward. By the time I finished reading through it, I wasn't just ready to take on the project—I was excited to prove to myself that I was capable of more than I was giving myself credit for.

But postpartum wasn't the only time I leaned on my Confidence Resume. Early in my career, I found myself struggling with a similar crisis of confidence. I had just transitioned into a leadership role, and I was tasked with leading a high-profile client presentation. This was the kind of presentation that could make or break a career. I spent hours preparing, running through every detail, yet the night before, I was gripped by self-doubt. *What if they don't take me seriously? What if I stumble over my words? What if I fail?*

In a moment of desperation, I pulled out my Confidence Resume. At that point, it wasn't as long or detailed as it is now, but it included enough to make me pause and reflect. There it was: the time I had spearheaded a team project that exceeded our revenue goals. The moment I had handled a tough client negotiation with professionalism and poise. The time I had been promoted ahead of schedule because of my ability to deliver results. These weren't just random achievements—they were proof that I had faced challenges before and come out stronger. And if I had done it then, why couldn't I do it now?

The next day, I walked into that presentation with my Confidence Resume playing on a mental loop. Did I still feel a few nerves? Absolutely. But I also felt grounded in the knowledge of my own capabilities. The presentation went better than I could have hoped, and I left the room not only with a happy client but also with a renewed belief in myself.

Creating your own Confidence Resume is a practice of self-acknowledgment. It's a way to visually see your strengths and remind yourself of the times when you've overcome obstacles. This list isn't just a record of the past; it's a source of strength that you can lean on when self-doubt creeps in.

Take some time to start your own. Begin with the big moments—career milestones, personal achievements, or challenges you've conquered. Then, add the smaller wins that make you smile, like sticking to a goal you set or receiving kind feedback from a colleague. Over time, your Confidence Resume will grow into a powerful tool—a living, breathing reminder of your resilience and capability. Whether you're navigating a tough season or stepping into a new challenge, it's there to remind you of everything you've already accomplished—and of everything you're capable of achieving.

Steps to Create Your Confidence Resume

1. **List Every Win:** Take some time to reflect on your life and write down every accomplishment you can remember. Don't overthink it—this exercise is about recognizing your wins, not judging their size or significance. Remember, nothing is too big or too small for this list. The moments that make you feel proud, no matter how simple they may seem, are the ones that build the foundation of your confidence.

Start by thinking about the major milestones in your life—those big moments when you knew you had accomplished something meaningful. These could be professional achievements like landing a promotion, launching a project, or switching careers. Or they could be personal triumphs, like overcoming a health challenge, learning to cook a new dish, helping a friend through a tough time, starting a family, or running your first race.

But don't stop there. Dig deeper. Think about the smaller victories that might not seem as flashy but still hold weight in your journey. Maybe it's the time you stood up for yourself in a difficult conversation or the day you finally completed that online course you'd been putting off. Perhaps it's learning to drive, sticking to a fitness routine, or even planting your first garden.

I'll share a peek at my own list to help you get started. It includes things like getting a job that allows me to work from home and travel, earning my master's degree in three semesters, running three half marathons, spending quality time with my mother when she was in the hospital after an accident, getting married, volunteering in a women's organization, buying my first house, giving birth to my son, maintaining long-distance friendships, leading a big team project in my MBA program, and even going skiing for the first time. I've also included things like winning a fitness competition (twice!) and taking golf lessons. Some are big, some are small—but every single one holds meaning in my life.

This list is for you. Be generous with yourself. Write down everything that comes to mind, even if you think it seems insignificant. You'll be surprised at how these moments add up to tell the story of your resilience, growth, and strength. The goal here isn't to create a perfect list—it's to remind yourself of all the ways you've shown up, worked hard, and triumphed in your own unique way.

2. **Identify Themes:** As you review your list, take a moment to look for patterns or themes. These aren't just random achievements—they're a reflection of your unique strengths and the qualities that define who you are. Maybe you notice that many of your wins came from persevering through tough times. That tells you something powerful about your resilience. Or perhaps your list highlights moments where you connected deeply with others—proof that you have a natural gift for building relationships. You might see examples of creative problem-solving, a love for adventure, or a talent for leading others through challenging situations.

   Pause and ask yourself: *What do these wins say about me?* By analyzing your past successes, you'll start to see recurring themes that reveal your core strengths. These aren't just the building blocks of your confidence; they're the traits you can rely on time and time again, no matter what life throws your way.

   I'll give you an example from my own list. When I reflected on my Confidence Resume, I noticed a theme of persistence. Whether it was completing my master's degree in three semesters, training for half marathons, or navigating the ups and downs of long-distance friendships, I saw a pattern of sticking with things, even when they were hard. That realization gave me a renewed sense of confidence. It reminded me that I can face challenges because I've done it before—and I can do it again.

   This exercise isn't just about celebrating what you've done; it's about recognizing the unique strengths that make you who you are. When you understand what you bring to the table, you can approach new challenges with a renewed sense of confidence. These themes are your personal guideposts, showing you how to tap into your strengths when you need them most.

3. **Make It Visible:** Place your Confidence Resume somewhere you'll see it regularly. Think about the spaces you spend the most time in—your desk, your journal, your planner, or even as a note saved on your phone. Having this reminder nearby will help reinforce your self-belief, especially on days when self-doubt starts to creep in. Imagine glancing over at your Confidence Resume before a big meeting or during a tough moment. It's like having a pep talk from the most capable version of yourself.

   Here's what works for me: I keep my Confidence Resume right next to my desk, alongside some of my favorite inspirational quotes. It's my go-to when I need a quick confidence boost or a reminder of everything I've accomplished. Seeing it often keeps those wins fresh in my mind and gives me the motivation to tackle whatever comes my way.

   Your Confidence Resume is more than a list; it's a tool for encouragement. By keeping it visible, you're giving yourself daily reminders of your resilience and capability—and that's a powerful thing.

4. **Revisit and Update Regularly:** Confidence is a journey, not a one-time destination, and your accomplishments are always evolving. That's why it's important to revisit and update your Confidence Resume regularly. Life moves quickly, and it's easy to overlook the incredible things you achieve along the way. Set a reminder to check in with your resume every few months. Treat it like a celebration—a dedicated time to pause, reflect, and acknowledge the progress you've made.

   When you revisit your Confidence Resume, don't just skim over the list. Take a moment to really reflect on each addition. Think about what it took to reach that milestone—whether it was persistence, creativity, or sheer determination. Each win, no matter the size, is a testament to your growth and resilience.

This is also the perfect time to tie it back to the weekly wins you've started keeping track of from Chapter 1. Flip through your wins list and ask yourself, *What stands out? What deserves a spot on my Confidence Resume?* Maybe it's a major career achievement, like leading a successful project. Or maybe it's something more personal, like creating a new habit or showing up for someone when they needed you.

Your Confidence Resume is a living document, one that grows and evolves alongside you. Revisit it often, and let it remind you of your ability to navigate challenges and continue pushing forward. By keeping it updated, you're not just recording your successes—you're actively reinforcing your belief in what you're capable of achieving.

Confidence in Your Unique Journey

As you create your Confidence Resume, remember that your journey is uniquely yours. There's no need to compare your accomplishments to anyone else's. Confidence isn't about checking off a universal list of achievements or striving for a resume that looks like someone else's highlight reel. It's about recognizing and celebrating the strengths that make you who you are.

Take a moment to reflect on that. Your experiences, challenges, and triumphs are yours alone. The journey of building self-belief is deeply personal, and every achievement—no matter how big or small—adds to your story. Whether it's earning a degree, navigating a career change, or simply finding joy in your day-to-day life, each moment of pride is a thread in the tapestry of your unique journey.

I'll share something that took me a while to learn. Early in my career, I would look at colleagues who seemed to have it all together—promotions, accolades, even perfect family photos on social media—and I'd feel like I was falling behind. Their paths seemed so polished, while mine felt messy, full of detours and second-guessing. But over time, I realized that their accomplishments didn't take away from mine. My wins were no less valid just because they looked different. In fact, it was in those moments of self-reflection that I found the courage to embrace my journey, messiness, and all.

Your Confidence Resume isn't about striving for perfection; it's about documenting your growth and honoring the person you're becoming. Each entry on your list represents not just what you've achieved, but the courage it took to get there. It's a reminder of your resilience, your ability to overcome obstacles, and your commitment to showing up for yourself—even when it's hard.

Here's something to try: Each time you revisit your Confidence Resume, pick one accomplishment and really reflect on it. Ask yourself, *What did it take for me to achieve this? What strengths did I rely on?* Write those reflections down alongside the accomplishment. Over time, you'll see patterns emerge—qualities like perseverance, creativity, or adaptability. These are your core strengths, the ones you can lean on as you continue to grow.

One of the most beautiful things about confidence is that it isn't static—it evolves. The more you honor your journey, the more self-belief you cultivate. And the more self-belief you cultivate, the more equipped you are to face life's challenges with purpose and grace.

So, as you create and revisit your Confidence Resume, take a moment to honor the person you are becoming. Don't rush past the wins or dismiss them as unimportant. Each accomplishment, no matter how small, is a building block in the foundation of your confidence.

Together, they tell the story of a woman who is capable, resilient, and uniquely equipped to create the life she desires.

Remember: Your journey is yours.
And that's what makes it so powerful.

Grab your journal and reflect on these questions:

- What are the significant moments in your life that make you feel proud?

- What professional milestones did you achieve?

- What personal triumphs have you overcome?

- What small victories have you had that made a big impact on your self-belief?

- What themes emerge as you reflect on the accomplishments you've had over the years?

Access the free workbook by scanning the QR code:

https://www.amandacahill.com/redefiningyouresources

Key Takeaways on Redefining Your Accomplishments

- **Acknowledging Your Wins Builds Confidence**: Confidence is strengthened when you take time to recognize and celebrate your past achievements, both big and small. Every success is a testament to your resilience, growth, and capabilities.

- **Society Conditions Us to Downplay Success**: Many of us are taught to minimize our accomplishments to appear humble, but this habit erodes confidence. True humility lies in appreciating your strengths and owning your hard work, not dismissing them.

- **Flipping the Script Empowers You**: Instead of brushing off compliments or attributing achievements to luck, practice saying, "Thank you, I worked hard on that." Acknowledging your wins creates space for self-belief and encourages others to celebrate themselves, too.

- **The Confidence Resume as a Transformative Tool**: A Confidence Resume is a personal list of your accomplishments, from career milestones to small, meaningful victories. It serves as a reminder of your strengths and can be revisited whenever self-doubt creeps in.

- **Wins Come in All Sizes**: Milestones like promotions and personal achievements like running your first race or learning a new skill are equally valuable in your journey. Both types of wins contribute to your confidence and tell a story of perseverance.

- **Themes in Accomplishments Reflect Your Core Strengths**: Reviewing your Confidence Resume can reveal patterns, like resilience, creativity, or adaptability. These themes highlight your unique qualities and become guideposts for future challenges.

- **Visibility Reinforces Self-Belief**: Keep your Confidence Resume in a place where you'll see it often, such as your desk or journal. This practice serves as a daily reminder of your capabilities and bolsters your confidence in moments of doubt.

- **Update Your Resume Regularly**: Confidence is a journey, not a one-time event. Revisit and update your Confidence Resume often to celebrate new achievements and reflect on your ongoing growth.

- **Your Journey Is Unique**: Confidence isn't about comparing yourself to others; it's about recognizing the strengths and accomplishments that make you who you are. Each person's path is different, and your wins are valid, no matter their size or form.

- **Celebrate Yourself to Inspire Others**: By embracing your own accomplishments, you become a role model for others to do the same. Confidence built on self-recognition is unshakable and empowers those around you to own their stories as well.

CHAPTER 3

Redefine Your Beliefs

"You have been criticizing yourself for years, and it hasn't worked. Try approving of yourself and see what happens." – Louise Hay

Life has a way of filling our minds with noise—the "shoulds" and "shouldn'ts," the limitations, and the stories we've been told about who we are. Over time, these narratives take root, shaping how we see ourselves and the possibilities for our lives. It's easy to let these limiting beliefs become our truth, making us feel small, undeserving, or not enough. But here's the powerful reality: those beliefs—the ones that whisper what you can't do—aren't facts. They're simply thoughts. And thoughts can be changed.

I know this because I've lived it. For years, I carried around beliefs that whispered constantly in the back of my mind: *You're not enough. You'll never be enough.* I wasn't talented enough to achieve my goals, likable enough to build deep, lasting friendships, or worthy enough to create the life I secretly dreamed about. These beliefs weren't fleeting doubts that came and went; they felt like permanent truths etched into my identity. They were the lens through which I saw myself and the world around me. Because I believed them so deeply, they shaped how I moved through life—hesitant, second-guessing every decision, playing small, and quietly shrinking away from opportunities that felt just beyond my grasp.

I rarely admitted these feelings to anyone, not even to myself. Instead, I buried them beneath a facade of competence and busyness, hoping that if I worked hard enough or achieved enough, they might disappear. But no matter how much I accomplished, that gnawing sense of unworthiness lingered, like a shadow I couldn't escape. I didn't just doubt myself—I doubted that I even had the right to want more or something different.

I remember one evening that changed everything. I was sitting alone on the couch, scrolling mindlessly through social media. My feed was a cascade of perfect moments: women celebrating promotions, sharing snapshots of deep, joyful friendships, or posing in front of stunning backdrops from their latest adventures. They seemed so vibrant, so bold, so confident in who they were and what they were capable of. Meanwhile, I was sitting there in silence, feeling the weight of my own inadequacy. My chest tightened, and a knot formed in my stomach. My mind raced with thoughts like, *How does she have it all figured out? Why does this seem so easy for her? What's wrong with me?*

And then, like a quiet voice cutting through the noise, came the thought that I couldn't ignore: *Why not me?* It wasn't loud or dramatic, but it was heavy, and it stayed with me. It wasn't just a question—it was an accusation; one I couldn't explain away. For so long, I had blamed my circumstances or told myself that other people were simply luckier, more talented, or more deserving. But in that moment, it hit me: the biggest thing holding me back wasn't my circumstances. It wasn't my lack of talent or resources. It was me. It was the story I had been telling myself about who I was and what I deserved. And that story was suffocating me.

I wish I could say that realization led to an immediate transformation, but it didn't. Instead, it cracked something open inside me—a tiny, fragile space where the possibility of something different began to grow. I started to wonder: *What if I'm wrong about myself?* What if all these years of believing I wasn't enough had been a lie? What if I could change the story in my head and, in doing so, change my life? What if I actually was worthy of love, success, and joy? Those questions cracked open a door in my mind that I had kept locked for far too long. They allowed me to imagine new possibilities for my life—possibilities rooted in abundance, self-belief, and a deep sense of worthiness.

That was the moment I decided to redefine my beliefs. I told myself, *If I want to become the woman I've always dreamed of being, I have to change the way I think about myself.* This shift wasn't instantaneous or easy, but it was necessary. I had to start somewhere, and for me, that began with questioning the narratives I had been carrying for so long.

Redefining my beliefs wasn't just about changing my mindset—it was about reclaiming my power. The stories I had been telling myself about lack and unworthiness were keeping me stuck, but the moment I chose to rewrite them, everything began to shift. I started to see myself as someone capable of growth, resilience, and success. I began to trust in my ability to navigate challenges, and I allowed myself to dream bigger than I ever had before.

This process taught me a powerful lesson: Confidence doesn't come from perfection or the absence of fear. It comes from the courage to rewrite the story in your mind and step into the woman you were always meant to be. It's about recognizing that your worth isn't tied to anyone else's expectations or achievements—it's inherent, unshakable, and yours to claim.

If you've been carrying limiting beliefs, I want you to know that you're not alone. But I also want you to know that those beliefs don't define you. You have the power to change them. It starts with a decision—a quiet but courageous choice to challenge the thoughts that have held you back. It starts with asking, *What if I'm wrong about myself?* and opening your heart to the possibility of something greater.

When you redefine your beliefs, you're not just shifting your mindset—you're transforming your life. You're creating space for joy, connection, and purpose. You're stepping into the version of yourself you've always known you could be. And you're proving, day by day, that you are more than enough.

The Power of Inner Dialogue

One of the most critical shifts you can make in this process of redefining your beliefs is learning to listen to—and, ultimately, change—your inner dialogue. This is the quiet voice that narrates your days, shaping how you see yourself, your worth, and your potential. For many of us, that voice tends to be critical, doubtful, or downright harsh. The words it whispers—*You're not good enough. You'll never figure this out. You're failing*—become the stories we believe about ourselves. And here's the heartbreaking truth: We let that voice run unchecked, living rent-free in our minds, while it chips away at our confidence and self-worth.

I want you to pause for a moment and think about some of the things you say to yourself about yourself. *I'm so disorganized. I always mess things up. I'll never be as good as [insert comparison here].* Now, imagine saying those same things to someone you love—a best friend, your partner, or even your child. Can you picture looking into their eyes and saying, "You're a failure. You're not good enough. You'll never figure this out"? Of course not. So why is it that we allow ourselves to say those things internally, day after day? Isn't it crazy how much power we give to those words, even though we'd never speak them aloud to someone we care about?

The truth is, your inner dialogue is like the soil where your mindset grows. If that soil is filled with negativity and doubt, it will only produce more of the same. But when you start to plant seeds of self-love, encouragement, and possibility, something incredible happens: your mindset begins to transform. It's not about ignoring reality or pretending challenges don't exist. It's about choosing to speak to yourself in ways that uplift and empower you, even on the hard days.

Let me take you back to that sunny afternoon when I broke down to my husband. Up until that moment, my inner dialogue had been relentless. I was telling myself that I wasn't a good mom, that I didn't know what I was doing, and that I was failing in every aspect of my life. Every thought was laced with judgment and criticism, and it was exhausting. I didn't even realize how much damage I was doing to myself by allowing those thoughts to take root. But as I worked through that season, I began to utilize tools I had learned along the way to reshape my inner dialogue.

I started small. When the thought, *You're a terrible mom* surfaced, I paused and challenged it. Was it true? Of course not. I was doing the best I could, showing up for my son every day with love and care. So instead, I replaced it with, *I'm learning as I go, and I'm giving my son everything I have.* At first, it felt forced, even unnatural. But the more I practiced, the more those new thoughts began to feel like truth.

This process isn't about erasing negativity altogether. Life is hard, and challenges are real. But it is about flipping the script. It's about choosing to rewrite the narrative that plays in your mind. Imagine waking up in the morning, and instead of thinking, *I can't handle this day,* you tell yourself, *I'm capable of figuring this out.* Imagine replacing, *I'll never be good enough,* with, *I'm learning and growing every day.* These shifts might seem small, but over time, they add up in a big way.

Think about the power of perspective. Two people can face the same challenge, but their inner dialogue can lead to completely different outcomes. One person might think, *I can't do this; I'll never succeed,* and give up before they've even started. The other might think, *This is tough, but I'll take it one step at a time,* and persevere. The difference isn't in their abilities—it's in the way they speak to themselves.

Your inner dialogue has the power to shape how you show up in the world. When you choose to be kind, encouraging, and compassionate toward yourself, you cultivate a mindset of self-belief and resilience.

That shift doesn't just change the way you think—it changes the way you live.

Here's something to try: The next time you catch yourself in a spiral of negative self-talk, pause and ask yourself, *Is this true? Is this thought helping me, or is it holding me back?* Then, replace it with a statement rooted in self-love and possibility. It might feel awkward at first but don't underestimate the power of repetition. The more you practice, the more natural it becomes.

This isn't about perfection—it's about progress. It's about building a habit of speaking to yourself with the same kindness and encouragement you would offer to someone you love. Your inner dialogue has been shaping your life all along. Now, it's time to take control of that conversation and let it guide you toward the person you're becoming.

The 3 P's Method for Daily Mottos

One powerful way to anchor positive self-talk is through daily mottos. These are simple, affirming statements you repeat to yourself each day—reminders of who you are and who you are becoming. I first learned about mottos through Sarah Centrella, and they have been a game-changer in my journey. On days when self-doubt feels overwhelming, or the challenges of life seem too big, my mottos are like a lifeline, pulling me back to a place of belief and possibility. They remind me of the woman I'm working to become, even when I don't quite feel like her yet.

Creating effective mottos doesn't have to be complicated. By working through Sarah's method, I began to see a pattern: the mottos that helped me along my journey were using a **3 P's Method**—Personal, Present, and Positive—and it's an incredible framework to help you craft mottos that truly resonate and empower you.

Personal: Your daily mottos should resonate deeply with your values and your vision for the future. What do you need to hear today? What encouragement would help you step into the version of yourself you're striving to become? For example, when I was navigating a tough season in my life, my personal motto became, "I am worthy of love and joy." At the time, it felt aspirational, almost out of reach, but it spoke directly to the areas where I needed growth and healing. Over time, repeating that statement helped me internalize it as truth.

Present: State your mottos in the present tense, as if they are already true. Instead of saying, "I will be confident," say, "I am confident." This simple shift allows your mind to start believing in the reality of these statements. Our brains don't know the difference between imagined and real; they respond to what we consistently tell them. Speaking in the present tense sets the tone for your actions to align with the belief.

Positive: Focus on what you want to grow in your life, not what you want to avoid. Negative framing reinforces the challenges you're trying to overcome, but positive statements focus on the outcomes you're striving for. For example, instead of saying, "I'm not afraid," say, "I am courageous." This subtle shift emphasizes strength and possibility, helping you move toward a more empowered mindset.

Here are a few examples of daily mottos using the 3 P's method:

- "I am worthy of every success and every joy that comes my way."

- "I am strong enough to handle whatever challenges today brings."

- "I am becoming the woman I've always envisioned, one step at a time."

- "I am confident, capable, and deserving of the life I desire."

The beauty of daily mottos is that they are completely customizable. You can create mottos that fit your current season of life, the challenges you're facing, or the goals you're pursuing. The key is to choose statements that feel meaningful to you—words that lift you up and keep you aligned with the future you're working toward.

Practicing Your Mottos

Creating mottos is only the first step. The real power comes from weaving them into your daily life. Take a few minutes each morning to speak your mottos out loud or write them down. The act of saying them out loud reinforces their truth, even if it feels uncomfortable at first. If you want to take this practice to the next level, try standing in front of a mirror and speaking your mottos directly to yourself. Look yourself in the eyes as you say the words. It may feel awkward, even silly, the first few times, but stick with it. There's something incredibly powerful about speaking your truth while looking yourself in the eyes—it's a declaration of self-belief.

When I first started practicing mirror affirmations, I couldn't look at myself without feeling self-conscious. My inner dialogue would pipe up with critiques: *You don't really believe this. Who are you kidding?* But I kept showing up, day after day. Slowly, the discomfort faded, and in its place came a sense of connection and confidence. Now, it's one of my favorite rituals. It's not just about the words—it's about claiming them as my truth.

How Mottos Anchor Your Growth

Daily mottos are more than just words—they are guideposts. They anchor you when life feels chaotic, reminding you of your vision and your potential. They help you shift your focus from doubt to belief, from fear to possibility. With every repetition, you're training your mind to see yourself not as who you've been, but as who you are becoming.

Mottos also serve as a powerful tool for realignment. When you face setbacks or challenges, returning to your mottos can help you refocus on what matters most. They act as a reminder that growth is a process and that confidence is built one thought, one belief, and one action at a time.

As you begin creating and practicing your own daily mottos, remember this: They are an extension of your inner dialogue. The words you choose have power, and by using them intentionally, you are building the foundation for the woman you are becoming. Speak them with conviction, even on the days you don't feel their truth yet. Trust that, over time, these mottos will not just shape your thoughts—they will shape your life.

Embracing "What If"

One of the greatest barriers to redefining your beliefs is fear—the fear of failure, the fear of judgment, the fear of stepping into the unknown. Fear has a sneaky way of keeping us stuck, convincing us that it's safer to stay small, avoid risk, and settle for less than we're capable of. But what if, instead of letting fear drive your decisions, you chose to ask yourself one simple question: *What if everything goes right?*

Too often, we stop ourselves from dreaming big because we're consumed by worst-case scenarios. Our minds love to play out every possible way things could go wrong: *What if I fail? What if people judge me? What if I'm not good enough?* These thoughts feel protective, like they're shielding us from disappointment, but in truth, they're just building walls around our potential.

Now, imagine flipping the script. Instead of asking, *What if I fail?* ask, *What if I succeed?* What if you actually could create the life you've always dreamed of? What if you broke through the barriers you've placed on yourself and succeeded in ways you never thought possible? What if stepping into the unknown led to the greatest growth and joy of your life? This is the power of embracing the "What If" mindset. It's not about ignoring fear or pretending challenges don't exist—it's about choosing to focus on what's possible instead of what could go wrong. It's about imagining the best-case scenario and letting that vision guide your actions.

I'll never forget the fear I felt when I first thought about starting a podcast. It had been in my heart for years—this vision of creating a space to share stories, inspire others, and build a community. But every time I considered taking the first step, the fear crept in. *What if nobody listens? What if people judge me? What if I can't figure out the technology? What if I put myself out there, and it's a complete failure?* Those thoughts were loud, relentless, and convincing. I let them stop me time and time again.

Every time I started researching equipment or brainstorming ideas, I'd find an excuse to put it off. I told myself I wasn't ready, that I needed to learn more, plan more, or wait for the "right time." Deep down, though, I knew the real problem wasn't a lack of knowledge or preparation—it was fear. I was terrified of failing, of being judged, of stepping into the unknown and not measuring up.

Then, one day, I decided to ask myself a different question: *What if it works? What if this podcast becomes the thing that changes everything for me? What if it helps me connect with people in ways I never imagined? What if it brings me joy, growth, and fulfillment?* That shift in perspective didn't erase the fear, but it quieted it enough for me to take the first step. I bought the equipment. I recorded my first episode. And when I finally hit publish, it wasn't perfect, but it was a start.

Looking back now, I can't imagine what my life would be like if I had let fear win. That podcast has brought me connections, opportunities, and a sense of purpose that I never would have experienced if I hadn't embraced the "What If" mindset. It wasn't just about launching a podcast—it was about proving to myself that I was capable of stepping into the unknown and succeeding.

The "What If" mindset isn't just about thinking positively; it's about taking action. Once you allow yourself to dream big, the next question becomes: *If I were already the woman I've always wanted to be, what would I do differently today?* Would you finally start the project you've been putting off? Would you make decisions based on confidence and trust in yourself rather than hesitation and self-doubt? Whatever it is, start doing it now. Even small steps create momentum. Each action you take from a place of possibility brings you closer to the version of yourself you're striving to become.

The beauty of the "What If" mindset is that it's not just a one-time exercise; it's a habit you can cultivate. Each time fear threatens to hold you back, pause and ask yourself: *What's the best that could happen?* Picture the doors that could open, the connections you could make, and the joy you could experience. Let those possibilities guide your actions.

Fear will always be part of the process—it's a natural reaction to stepping outside your comfort zone. But when you embrace the "What If" mindset, fear loses its power to control your choices. Instead, you start making decisions based on hope, belief, and the limitless possibilities that lie ahead. The life you want is on the other side of the fears that hold you back. And with each small step you take, you're proving to yourself that those fears don't define you. You have the power to create something extraordinary—it all starts with the courage to ask, *What if everything goes right?*

Redefine Your Beliefs, Redefine Your Life

Redefining your beliefs isn't a quick fix; it's a process, a journey of discovery and growth. It's about reclaiming the power to decide what you believe about yourself and your potential. By transforming your inner dialogue, adopting daily mottos, and embracing the "What If" mindset, you can begin to shed the limiting beliefs that have held you back for far too long.

Remember this: You are far more capable, loved, and powerful than you realize. The life you've dreamed of isn't just possible—it's waiting for you. Take this moment to reflect on how far you've already come and honor the woman you are becoming. Your journey is unique, and your transformation is only just beginning.

Grab your journal and reflect on these questions:

- What are three mottos you can start using today to move you closer to the woman you want to become?

- What if you shifted your thoughts to focus on the best-case scenario? How would that change your life?

- If you were already the woman you've always wanted to be, what would you do differently today? How would you speak to yourself?

- Where are you letting fear hold you back?

  Access the free workbook by scanning the QR code:

https://www.amandacahill.com/redefiningyouresources

Key Takeaways on Redefining Your Beliefs

- **Beliefs Are Not Facts**: The limiting beliefs you carry—those whispering what you can't do—are not truths. They're simply thoughts shaped by past experiences, and you have the power to change them.

- **Your Inner Story Shapes Your Life**: The narratives you tell yourself about who you are and what you deserve influence how you show up in the world. Rewriting those stories can unlock possibilities you've never imagined.

- **The Turning Point: "Why Not Me?"**: The moment you question limiting beliefs and ask, "What if I'm wrong about myself?" is the moment transformation begins. This shift cracks open the door to self-belief and abundance.

- **Confidence Comes from Courage, Not Perfection**: True confidence isn't the absence of fear; it's the willingness to rewrite the story in your mind and take action despite uncertainty.

- **Inner Dialogue Shapes Mindset**: Negative self-talk erodes confidence, while positive, empowering inner dialogue builds resilience. Challenge harmful thoughts by asking, "Is this true?" and replacing them with affirming beliefs.

- **Daily Mottos Anchor Self-Belief**: Using the 3 P's Method—Personal, Present, and Positive—you can create daily mottos that reinforce the person you're becoming. For example, "I am confident, capable, and deserving of success."

- **Repetition Solidifies Growth**: Practice daily mottos by speaking them out loud or writing them down. Even if it feels awkward at first, this habit creates new, empowering patterns in your mindset.

- **Embrace the "What If" Mindset**: Shift from asking "What if I fail?" to "What if everything goes right?" Dream big, and let the vision of success guide your actions, even in the face of fear.

- **Fear Does Not Define You**: Fear is a natural part of growth, but it loses its power when you choose to act based on hope and possibility. Each step forward builds momentum and courage.

- **Redefining Beliefs Transforms Your Life**: By changing how you think about yourself, you create space for joy, connection, and purpose. The journey isn't about perfection—it's about progress and stepping into the woman you've always been capable of becoming.

CHAPTER 4

The Strength Within

"You are more powerful than you know; you are beautiful just as you are." – Melissa Etheridge

Confidence isn't just about what you've achieved; it's also about understanding and embracing the unique qualities that make you who you are. Each of us possesses a blend of strengths, talents, and experiences that shape how we show up in the world. But how often do we pause to truly recognize and celebrate these qualities? When you take the time to reflect on and own what makes you uniquely you, you're building a foundation of self-assurance that's grounded in authenticity. This kind of confidence isn't fleeting—it's deeply rooted and unshakable.

For so many of us, the idea of owning our unique qualities feels foreign because we've spent much of our lives chasing validation from others. It starts young. We learn which behaviors and traits earn praise—being helpful, achieving good grades, being a "good girl," excelling in sports— and which ones are dismissed or criticized–talking too much, giggling, not being able to sit still. Over time, we begin to shape ourselves around what others find acceptable, hiding or downplaying the parts of us that don't fit into their expectations.

I know this trap all too well because I lived it. For years, I was praised for being driven and successful, for checking off milestones like earning promotions and achieving professional recognition. On paper, I looked like someone who had it all together. But inside, I felt an unsettling disconnect. I had spent so much time excelling in my career and meeting societal expectations that I had lost sight of my own values and passions. It was as if I was living according to a script someone else had written—

polished and impressive, but completely detached from the woman I truly was.

I remember one particular moment when this realization hit me hard. I was sitting in a meeting, surrounded by colleagues who were all striving for the same goals—bigger deals, higher numbers, more recognition. And I thought to myself, *Is this what I want? Or is this just what I think I should want?* That question stayed with me, quietly gnawing at the edges of my carefully constructed identity. I realized I had spent so much energy trying to live up to an external standard of success that I had never stopped to define what success meant to me.

Rediscovering my unique strengths became a turning point. I began to look at the qualities that had always been there but that I had overlooked or undervalued. My creativity, my ability to connect deeply with people, my passion for helping others grow—these were the parts of me that felt authentic and aligned. They weren't always the qualities that earned the loudest applause, but they were the ones that felt most true.

As I leaned into these strengths, I started to see confidence differently. It wasn't something I had to earn from others. It wasn't about being the smartest person in the room or achieving the most impressive title. Confidence came from embracing the fullness of who I was—from celebrating the quirks, passions, and talents that made me unique. When I stopped chasing external validation and started trusting my own voice, everything changed.

This chapter is an invitation to take that same journey. It's about breaking free from the trap of seeking validation and beginning the work of truly owning your unique qualities. You'll learn how to recognize the strengths you may have overlooked, how to embrace the parts of yourself you've been hiding, and how to shift your focus from external approval to internal alignment.

This isn't always an easy process. It requires honesty, reflection, and the courage to step away from the expectations you've been carrying. But it's also incredibly liberating. When you own who you are—fully and unapologetically—you unlock a kind of confidence that no one can take away. Because confidence isn't about becoming someone else; it's about coming home to yourself.

Recognizing Your Unique Strengths

The first step to owning your unique qualities is identifying them. Start by asking yourself: *What are the traits that make me who I am? What are the strengths that come naturally to me?* These might include qualities like empathy, resilience, creativity, or a knack for problem-solving. Take some time to think about these qualities and write them down. Often, the strengths we take for granted are the very ones that others admire in us—but because they come so naturally, we barely notice them.

I'll be honest: This wasn't an easy process for me at first. I used to struggle with identifying my strengths. I'd write down a couple of things—"hardworking" or "organized"—but it felt superficial. Then one day, someone suggested I ask people close to me for their perspective. I decided to give it a try, though I felt nervous about what they might say. What if they couldn't think of anything? What if I wasn't as capable as I hoped I was? But the responses I received were eye-opening.

A colleague told me they admired my ability to stay calm under pressure, something I'd never even considered a strength because it felt so normal to me. A friend mentioned how much they appreciated my knack for making people feel seen and heard. My husband shared that my determination to pursue my goals—even when they felt impossible— was one of the things that inspired him the most. Hearing these reflections not only gave me insights into my strengths but also helped me see myself in a way I never had before.

Exercises for Embracing Your Unique Qualities

1. **Strength Inventory:** Start by making a list of qualities and strengths that you believe define who you are. Write them down—yes, physically write them down. Seeing the words on paper makes them feel real and tangible. Include things like "I'm a good listener," "I'm adaptable," or "I have a strong sense of empathy." Don't let modesty hold you back—this is your moment to celebrate yourself unapologetically. If you feel stuck, think about compliments you've received in the past. What do people often thank you for? What comes easily to you that others might find challenging?

2. **External Perspectives:** Sometimes, we're too close to our own experiences to see ourselves clearly. We might downplay our accomplishments or overlook the strengths that others see in us. This is where the perspective of others becomes invaluable. Consider asking for feedback from people you trust—friends, colleagues, mentors, or family members. You can even engage in a 360-degree review, where you receive feedback from a diverse group of individuals who interact with you in different contexts. Ask them questions like:

   1. What do you see as my greatest strengths?

   2. What is unique or different about me that adds value?

   3. Where do you believe my confidence shines the brightest?

The feedback you receive can be incredibly affirming. It can help you see strengths you may have taken for granted or overlooked entirely. More importantly, it provides a fuller picture of your abilities and potential. This exercise isn't about seeking validation; it's about gaining insights that help you build authentic confidence.

When I first did this exercise, I wasn't sure what to expect. But the feedback I received completely shifted my perspective. One colleague pointed out that my ability to connect with people was a rare and valuable skill—something I had always brushed off as "just being friendly." Hearing it from someone else made me realize how much of an impact that quality had on my relationships and my work. Since then, I've made it a habit to revisit this exercise every couple of years, and each time, I walk away feeling more connected to my strengths.

Pro Tip: As you gather feedback, keep a record of it in a document or spreadsheet you can refer back to. I have a running list where I store everything from compliments and kudos emails to kind words from friends and clients. It's become a powerful resource for those days when I'm feeling uncertain, or my confidence is wavering. Just reading through those words reminds me of my values and helps me realign with my strengths.

3. **Celebrate Differences:** Think about a time when your unique qualities made a positive impact. Maybe your creativity helped solve a problem at work, or your empathy supported a friend in need. Reflecting on these moments reinforces the value of your strengths and helps you see how they contribute to the world.

For example, I once led a team project that was struggling to move forward because everyone had different priorities. I leaned into my strength of being a strong communicator and facilitator, organizing a brainstorming session that allowed everyone to feel heard and aligned with our goals. That one meeting turned everything around—and it reminded me how valuable my natural ability to bring people together really is.

When you start to recognize your strengths, you not only build confidence in yourself but also deepen your understanding of how you show up for others. Each strength is like a piece of the puzzle that makes you, *you*. Together, they create a unique picture that no one else can replicate.

Embrace Your Whole Self

Owning your unique qualities isn't just about celebrating your strengths; it's about embracing the entirety of who you are—imperfections and all. True confidence comes from accepting yourself fully, not just the polished, put-together parts you're proud to share with the world, but also the parts you might wish to hide. The parts you label as "flaws" or "weaknesses" often hold the most potential for growth. They shape your journey and help you become the person you are today.

For years, I struggled with the idea that being friendly and approachable might make me seem less capable. In a world that often equates authority with seriousness, I worried that my natural warmth—my tendency to smile, engage, and build relationships easily—might lead others to underestimate me. I convinced myself that if I wanted to be taken seriously, I had to dial it back, project a more rigid demeanor, and focus on being perceived as "all business." So, I tried. I walked into meetings with a serious face, kept conversations strictly professional, and resisted the urge to bring my natural energy into the room. But instead of feeling more powerful, I felt disconnected—like I was performing rather than leading.

It wasn't until I embraced my natural ability to connect with others that everything shifted. I realized that my warmth wasn't a weakness—it was a strength. My ability to build relationships, make people feel comfortable, and create an open dialogue made me more effective, not less. When I stopped suppressing who I was and started owning it, I saw that leadership isn't about fitting into a rigid mold—it's about showing up fully as yourself. By reframing this perceived flaw as an asset, I gained a deeper level of confidence—one rooted in authenticity and self-acceptance.

When you embrace your whole self—the strengths, the quirks, and even the qualities you once viewed as flaws—you're cultivating a confidence that is unshakable. This isn't a confidence dependent on external validation or approval. It's a confidence born from knowing who you are, honoring that truth, and showing up fully as yourself. Authentic confidence allows you to shed the need for pretense. It lets you stop wasting energy on trying to fit into someone else's mold or live up to their expectations. When you're rooted in who you are, you stop comparing your journey to others and start valuing the unique path you're on. It's freeing. It's powerful. And it's magnetic.

Once I stopped trying to suppress the parts of myself I deemed "unacceptable" and began to embrace them, everything changed. I stopped fearing rejection because I was no longer rejecting myself. I noticed how people responded differently to me when I showed up as my authentic self, unafraid to be vulnerable, quirky, or imperfect. It inspired deeper connections and gave others permission to be themselves, too.

Owning your unique qualities starts with embracing them fully—the good, the messy, the misunderstood. Confidence isn't about eliminating imperfections; it's about seeing them as part of what makes you beautifully human. And when you lean into the fullness of who you are, you unlock a confidence that no one can take away. You stop chasing perfection and start owning your power.

This type of confidence doesn't just transform how you see yourself. When you embrace your whole self and show up authentically, you give others permission to do the same. You become a source of inspiration, showing that confidence isn't about being flawless—it's about being real.

Confidence as a Journey

Confidence isn't a destination; it's a journey—a continuous process of learning, growing, and embracing yourself more fully each day. Some days, confidence will feel effortless, as though it's a natural part of you. Other days, it might feel like a struggle. That's okay. Each step you take toward self-acceptance strengthens the foundation of belief in yourself. Over time, those small, consistent steps create a resilient, authentic confidence that will carry you through life's challenges.

As you reflect on your unique qualities, remember that they are your superpowers. Your strengths, quirks, and passions are what make you, *you*. They are gifts not only to yourself but also to the world. When you show up fully as the person you are meant to be, you create a ripple effect. Your authenticity inspires others to embrace their own unique qualities. By owning who you are, you're leading by example—showing that confidence doesn't come from perfection but from embracing your perfectly imperfect self.

Take a moment to think about the parts of yourself you've been hesitant to embrace. What would it look like to view those qualities through a lens of acceptance and compassion? How might those so-called "flaws" actually be strengths in disguise?

I invite you to lean into the fullness of who you are—the parts you love, the parts you're still learning to accept, and the parts that make you wonderfully, uniquely *you*. Because the world doesn't need you to be perfect. It needs you to be authentic, confident, and unapologetically yourself.

Owning your unique strengths isn't just about building confidence— it's about creating a life that reflects your truth. And as you continue this journey, remember: When you embrace your whole self, you're not just empowering yourself; you're inspiring others to do the same.

Grab your journal and reflect on these questions:

- What are the traits that make you who you are? What are the strengths that come naturally to you?

- Who can you reach out to seek feedback on who you are and what you've done? (Make a list of 5–10 people)

- Ask them:

    o What do they see as your greatest strengths?

    o How have they seen you overcome challenges?

    o Where do they believe your confidence shines the brightest?

- What themes emerge as you reflect on your accomplishments and feedback?

- Are there parts of you that you hesitate to embrace? What would it look like to view those qualities through a lens of acceptance and compassion?

   Access the free workbook by scanning the QR code:

https://www.amandacahill.com/redefiningyouresources

Key Takeaways on Owning Your Unique Qualities

- **Confidence Is Grounded in Authenticity**: True confidence doesn't come from external achievements or validation—it's rooted in embracing the unique qualities, quirks, and strengths that make you who you are.

- **Validation Is a Trap**: Chasing external approval often leads to disconnection from your authentic self. Confidence flourishes when you stop seeking validation and begin aligning with your own values and passions.

- **Define Success on Your Terms**: Instead of following societal scripts or external expectations, take the time to reflect on what success truly means to you. Owning your journey requires stepping away from the "shoulds" and embracing what feels right for you.

- **Recognize and Celebrate Your Strengths**: Identify the traits and abilities that come naturally to you, such as empathy, creativity, or resilience. These strengths often feel ordinary to you but are extraordinary to others.

- **Gather External Perspectives**: Ask trusted friends, colleagues, or mentors for feedback on your strengths. Their insights can help you uncover qualities you've overlooked or undervalued.

- **Celebrate Your Differences**: Reflect on moments when your unique qualities made a positive impact. These experiences highlight the value of being your authentic self and reinforce the importance of leaning into your strengths.

- **Embrace Imperfections**: Confidence isn't about eliminating flaws; it's about embracing the entirety of who you are. What you perceive as weaknesses often hold hidden strengths and contribute to your growth.

- **Authenticity Is Magnetic**: When you stop fearing rejection and fully embrace your whole self, you inspire deeper connections and give others permission to show up authentically.

- **Confidence Is a Journey**: Confidence grows through consistent self-reflection, self-acceptance, and action. It's not a fixed destination but an ongoing process of becoming your best, most authentic self.

- **Your Uniqueness Is Your Superpower**: Your strengths, passions, and quirks are gifts to both yourself and the world. Owning them fully not only empowers you but also creates a ripple effect that inspires others to embrace their own uniqueness.

SECTION 2:
CREATING YOUR VISION

CHAPTER 5

Who Are You?

"Owning our story and loving ourselves through that process is the bravest thing we'll ever do."
– Brené Brown

You are a living, breathing, evolving woman. The woman you are today is made up of your experiences, your choices, and all the lessons you've learned along the way. She's strong, she's resilient, and she's more than capable of building the life she dreams of. And yet, there might be moments when you feel stuck, uncertain, or longing for change. That's not failure; that's growth calling. It's your inner compass pointing toward something more—a version of yourself you may not fully see yet but can feel deep within.

Before you can redefine yourself and become the woman you're meant to be, it's essential to pause and reflect on where you are right now. Think of it like planting a garden: You need to understand the soil before you can grow anything new. Taking inventory of yourself isn't about focusing on what's wrong. It's about celebrating how far you've come and identifying what's ready to grow. It's a process of acknowledging your strengths, your resilience, and the foundation of the life you're building.

I know this can feel uncomfortable. The thought of turning inward can be daunting, especially when we tend to see ourselves through such a critical lens. We magnify our mistakes, overlook our victories, and minimize the qualities that make us remarkable. But here's the truth: This process isn't about finding flaws or picking apart every imperfection. It's about seeing yourself fully, with compassion and curiosity. It's an act of love and care for yourself. You're not judging—you're honoring your journey.

When I first embarked on my personal development journey, I had no idea how difficult this kind of reflection could be. I remember working with an executive coach, someone I had turned to for guidance during a particularly chaotic season of my life. During one of our first sessions, she asked me a simple question: "What do you like about yourself?" The silence was deafening. My mind went blank, and I felt a lump rising in my throat as I held back tears. I couldn't think of a single thing to say. Tears spilled down my cheeks as I sat there, overwhelmed by the realization that I didn't know who I was anymore. It wasn't just that I couldn't find an answer—I couldn't even find the words to begin.

That moment was a wake-up call. I had spent so much time striving, achieving, and trying to meet everyone else's expectations that I had lost sight of myself entirely. The woman I thought I was had become a stranger to me. I didn't know what I valued, what I loved about myself, or who I wanted to be. It was a humbling moment, but it was also the beginning of something powerful.

As I started to work through this process, I realized that taking inventory wasn't about judging myself—it was about getting curious. I had to let go of the need to have all the answers and instead focus on asking the right questions. Questions like, "What do I like about myself?" That simple question, as difficult as it was, became a starting point for understanding who I was at my core.

This process wasn't quick, and it wasn't easy. There were days when I felt frustrated, convinced that I would never find the clarity I was searching for. But as I gave myself the time and space to reflect, the answers began to surface. I started to see myself more clearly—not through the critical lens I had been using for so long, but through a lens of compassion and truth. I realized that I was someone who cared deeply about others, someone who could find joy in the small things, and someone who had weathered life's storms with quiet strength. These weren't qualities I had ever celebrated before, but as I began to recognize them, I felt a spark of something I hadn't felt in a long time: pride.

Taking inventory of yourself requires courage because it asks you to confront the full picture of who you are. It asks you to look at the parts of yourself you're proud of and the parts you'd rather hide. But here's the magic: When you approach this process with honesty and compassion, you begin to see that even the parts of yourself you once viewed as flaws are part of what makes you beautifully human.

One of the hardest parts of this process for me was silencing the inner critic. That voice in my head was loud, relentless, and always quick to point out what I hadn't done or where I had fallen short. But I realized something powerful: The critic isn't the whole truth. Yes, I had made mistakes, but I had also learned from them. Yes, there were areas of my life that needed growth, but there were also areas where I was thriving.

As you embark on this journey of self-reflection, know that it's okay to feel uncomfortable. Growth often begins in discomfort. But give yourself permission to sit with those feelings and move through them, rather than running away. The answers you're looking for are already within you; they just need the space to be heard.

Imagine sitting in a quiet room, free from distractions. In front of you is a blank sheet of paper and a pen. You take a deep breath, close your eyes, and ask yourself: *What do I like about myself?* At first, the answers might come slowly. Maybe you write down something small, like, *I'm a good friend,* or *I have a great sense of humor.* But as you keep going, the list begins to grow. You start to remember moments when you felt proud of yourself—times when you showed up for someone in need, handled a challenge with grace, or simply allowed yourself to rest when you needed it most. These moments, big and small, are the building blocks of who you are today.

This process is about more than self-awareness—it's about self-celebration. The woman you are today is extraordinary, not because she's perfect, but because she's real. She's doing the best she can with what she has, and that's more than enough.

So, as you begin to take inventory, be gentle with yourself. Treat this process not as a chore, but as an opportunity to reconnect with the essence of who you are. You might be surprised by what you find. The woman you are today is strong, resilient, and capable. And she is the foundation for the incredible life you're about to create.

Self-Inventory

Let's start with the question that was hardest for me in my journey: *What do I like about myself?*

It sounds simple, doesn't it? But when you sit down and really ask yourself this question, it can feel like staring into a mirror you haven't looked at in years. For so many of us, the answer doesn't come easily. We've spent so much time focused on what we need to fix, improve, or change about ourselves that we've forgotten to notice what's already good and beautiful.

As I mentioned earlier, when I first tried to answer this question, I felt a wave of panic. My mind went blank, and the silence was deafening. All I could think about were the ways I'd fallen short—the times I'd been impatient, the moments when I felt like I wasn't enough, and the mistakes I couldn't seem to let go of. It took everything in me to push past those thoughts and ask myself: *But what do I like?*

I started small. I wrote down that I liked how much I care about my family, how I try to make the people around me feel seen and valued. Then I thought about how I always try to show up for my friends, even on my busiest days. As I kept going, the list began to grow. I realized I liked how I could find humor in hard moments and how I could stay calm under pressure. I even allowed myself to write things like how I liked the shape of my eyes and the way my smile was infectious. These were things I'd never given myself credit for before, but as they appeared on the page, I started to feel a flicker of pride.

Now it's your turn. Think about the woman you are today. I know it's easier to focus on what you don't like—our brains seem to be wired that way. But what if, just for a moment, you set aside the criticism and saw yourself through the eyes of someone who loves you? What would they say? Maybe they'd tell you how thoughtful you are or how your smile can light up a room. Maybe they'd point out how resourceful you are, how you always seem to have a solution when things go sideways. Or perhaps they'd remind you of your patience, your resilience, or the way you always know just what to say to make someone feel better.

If you're still struggling, start with the small things. Do you like the way you can turn a tough day around with your favorite song? Or how you always make sure to call your best friend on their birthday, no matter how busy you are? Do you love the color of your eyes, the way your hair falls on a good day, or how you have a knack for finding the perfect gift? The truth is, there's no wrong answer here. There's no achievement too small, no quality too insignificant to add to your list. The point is to give yourself permission to see yourself as the incredible, multifaceted woman you are.

Take a deep breath, find a quiet moment, and start writing. Let the words flow without judgment. Start small, and let your list grow naturally. With each new item, you're not just creating a list—you're building a bridge to self-compassion and pride. And trust me, you have so much to be proud of.

Another question to ask yourself:
What am I proud of?

When was the last time you truly sat with this question—not just for a fleeting moment, but long enough to let the answers sink in? If you're like most of us, it's probably been a while. We're so quick to move from one task to the next, from one goal to the next, that we rarely pause to acknowledge our wins. It's as though we've been taught that celebrating ourselves is indulgent or unnecessary. But here's the truth: recognizing what you're proud of isn't just a luxury—it's essential.

Maybe you've secured a job you once dreamed of, a role you used to only imagine yourself in. You've worked hard, grown through challenges, and shown up day after day to make it happen. But how often have you allowed yourself to sit back and say, _I'm proud of this. I made this happen_?

Perhaps your victories are quieter, but no less meaningful. Maybe you've cultivated a habit that brings you peace, like taking five minutes every morning to breathe deeply before the chaos of the day begins. Or maybe you've managed to maintain some semblance of balance in your busy life, carving out moments of joy even when the to-do list feels never-ending. These moments matter. They are the small but mighty building blocks of a life well-lived.

I remember a time when I was juggling so much—work deadlines, family commitments, and everything in between—that I felt like I was barely keeping my head above water. One evening, as my husband and I were tucking our son into bed, my husband looked at me and smiled as he said, "Today was the best day." My heart stopped. I hadn't done anything extraordinary that day—just spent time with him and our son, played a few games, and listened to our son babble as he played with his toys. In that moment, I realized how often I overlooked these kinds of wins. I had been so focused on what I wasn't doing, what I hadn't achieved, that I failed to recognize the quiet triumphs that mattered most.

What about you? What are the moments that make you proud? Maybe it's something big, like running a marathon or earning a degree. Or maybe it's the way you handled a difficult conversation with grace, the way you supported a friend in need, or the way you chose kindness in a moment of frustration. Big or small, every victory counts.

Take a moment to think about it now. Let yourself celebrate the things you've done, the obstacles you've overcome, and the progress you've made. Imagine how you'd feel if you allowed yourself to take credit for those moments, to see them as proof of your strength, determination, and growth. Here's the thing: Your wins don't have to be groundbreaking to be worth celebrating. Maybe you made it through a tough day with a smile, or maybe you remembered to take care of yourself when you needed it most. These moments matter because they are a reflection of who you are—a woman who is doing her best, learning, growing, and showing up, even when it's hard.

So, take a deep breath, and let the memories come. Write them down if you can. Feel free to refer back to some of the moments you captured in your Confidence Resume. Give yourself permission to honor the path you've walked, and let the pride settle in. You've worked hard to get here, and you deserve to acknowledge that. Because those victories, no matter how small they might seem, are the foundation of everything you're building.

Now, ask yourself:
Where am I feeling out of alignment?

This question isn't about finding faults or beating yourself up. It's about gently peeling back the layers of your life and noticing where things don't feel quite right. Think of it like tuning into the static on a radio—

you know there's a clearer signal, but something is interfering. Where in your life are you feeling resistance or dissatisfaction? Maybe it's your job. Perhaps it used to excite you, but now it leaves you feeling drained, like you're running on a treadmill with no finish line in sight. Or maybe it's a relationship that feels stagnant—a connection that once brought you joy but now feels like you're going through the motions. It could even be a habit, something small but persistent, that no longer serves you. Whatever it is, give yourself permission to name it.

Seeing these areas of misalignment isn't about judgment; it's about awareness. Imagine sitting across from a close friend as they vent about their struggles. You wouldn't criticize or dismiss them. You'd listen with empathy, offering encouragement and support. That's exactly how I want you to approach this question—with the same kindness and understanding you'd offer someone you love.

I remember a time when I felt completely out of alignment in my career. From the outside, everything looked fine—I had a great position, steady pay, and the respect of my peers. But inside? I felt stuck, like I was slowly shrinking in a role that didn't challenge or inspire me. Every Sunday night, a sense of dread would creep in as I thought about the week ahead. I tried to convince myself to be grateful, to focus on the positives. But the truth was, I wasn't living the life I wanted. I was living the life I thought I *should* want. It wasn't easy to admit that to myself. I wrestled with guilt—how could I feel this way when so many people would have loved to be in my shoes? But as I allowed myself to sit with those feelings, I realized they weren't there to make me feel bad. They were trying to tell me something. They were clues, showing me where I needed to grow, where I needed to make a change.

What about you? Where are you feeling resistance in your life? Maybe it's in the way you spend your time, or the way you show up in certain spaces. Maybe it's in a role you've outgrown or a dream you've been too afraid to chase. Wherever it is, take a moment to see it for what it is—a nudge from your inner self, pointing you toward something better. These moments of misalignment aren't roadblocks; they're guideposts. They're opportunities for you to pause, reflect, and ask yourself: *What would it look like to shift closer to the life I truly want?* The answers might not come all at once, and that's okay. The first step is simply noticing where things feel off and giving yourself the grace to explore why.

Remember, this isn't about tearing your life apart or starting over. It's about making adjustments, like realigning a crooked picture frame. Small shifts can have a big impact. Maybe it's setting a boundary in a relationship, exploring a new career path, or letting go of a habit that no longer serves you. Whatever it is, know that every step you take is a step closer to the life you deserve. Where are you feeling out of alignment? Sit with the question. Write it down. Let the answers come without judgment. They're not signs of failure—they're invitations to grow. And when you're ready, take that first step toward the clarity, fulfillment, and joy that alignment brings.

Another important question:
Who is the woman I am today?

It's a question that often gets lost in the noise of ambition, goals, and the constant striving to be better. We spend so much time focused on the woman we want to become that we rarely pause to appreciate the woman we already are. The woman you are today is the foundation for everything you're building. She deserves your attention, your love, and your gratitude.

So, who is she? What does she value? What matters most to her? Take a moment to think about it—not in terms of what she does, but in terms of who she is. This isn't about your roles, your to-do lists, or how much you've accomplished in the eyes of others. It's about your essence, your core. It's about the way you move through the world, the way you love, and the way you care for yourself.

I remember a time when I was so focused on the future version of myself—the woman who had it all figured out, who never doubted her worth, who seemed to glide through life effortlessly—that I completely overlooked the woman I was in that moment. She wasn't perfect, but she was trying. She was doing her best with what she had. And honestly? She was more than enough. But I didn't see it then. I was too busy measuring myself against impossible standards, thinking that I needed to be more, do more, achieve more. It wasn't until I hit a wall—burned out, overwhelmed, and questioning everything—that I finally stopped to ask myself: *Who am I right now?* The answer wasn't immediate, and it wasn't easy. At first, all I could see were the ways I fell short. But as I sat with the question, something began to shift. I started to notice the parts of myself I had been overlooking—the quiet strength I showed during hard times, the way I always tried to make people feel seen and valued, the resilience that kept me moving forward even when things felt impossible.

What about you? Who is the woman you are today? Maybe she's the kind of person who always finds a way to make others laugh, even on the hardest days. Maybe she's someone who values honesty, kindness, and connection. Maybe she's a fierce advocate for her loved ones, or maybe she's learning to set boundaries and prioritize her own needs. Whatever it is, it matters. It's what makes you, *you.* This is your reminder to give yourself credit for all the ways you show up—not just for others, but for yourself. Think about how you've handled life's challenges, the lessons you've learned, and the growth you've experienced. Even in the moments when you've felt unsure, you've kept going. That says so much about who you are. And let's not forget the way you care for yourself. Maybe it's as simple as making time for a morning cup of coffee, journaling before bed, or going for a walk to clear your head. These small acts of self-love are a testament to the woman you are today—a woman who is learning to honor herself, even in the midst of life's demands.

The truth is, you've got a lot going for you—more than you probably give yourself credit for. You're not just "enough"—you're extraordinary. The woman you are today has already overcome so much, learned so much, and grown so much. She's not a placeholder for your future self. She's a masterpiece in progress, and she's worthy of your love and appreciation right now. So, take a moment to sit with this question: *Who is the woman I am today?* Write it down if you can. Let the answers come naturally. And as you reflect, remind yourself of this: You are already more than enough.

As you take inventory, also consider the people in your life. **Who lifts you up, and who is holding you back?**

The people we surround ourselves with play an enormous role in shaping our confidence, our mindset, and our ability to grow. Relationships are meant to be a source of support and encouragement, but not all connections fulfill that purpose. Some people remind us of our worth, especially on the days when we forget it ourselves. These are your people—the ones who cheer you on, who challenge you to be better, and who love you unconditionally.

But then there are the other relationships—the ones that feel heavy, draining, or even toxic. Sometimes, taking stock of where you are in life means recognizing when it's time to set boundaries or let go of connections that no longer serve who you're becoming. That's not failure or betrayal; it's self-preservation. It's honoring the journey you're on and the woman you are striving to become.

Think about the people in your life who lift you up. Who are the ones who make you feel like you can take on the world? Maybe it's a close friend who always seems to know just what to say when you're doubting yourself, or a family member who has been your rock through life's toughest moments. These are the relationships worth cherishing. These are the people who see your potential even when you can't, and their love and encouragement are like a steady hand on your back, gently pushing you forward.

Now, think about the ones who might be holding you back. This isn't about casting blame or labeling someone as "bad." It's about being honest about the dynamics in your life. Maybe there's a colleague who constantly criticizes your ideas, a friend who seems to thrive on negativity, or a partner who doesn't support your growth. These relationships can create friction in your life, making it harder to move toward your goals.

For me, this process wasn't easy. I've always valued loyalty and connection, and the idea of distancing myself from certain people felt uncomfortable and even wrong at times. But there came a point when I realized that staying in relationships out of guilt or obligation was holding me back from the life I wanted. I had to make some tough choices—choices that weren't always understood by others but were necessary for my well-being. One of the most empowering lessons I've learned is this: *You are the director and starring role in the movie of your life.* You get to decide who stays in your story, who takes on a smaller role, and who no longer fits in with the narrative. That doesn't mean there's no love or respect for those you step away from—it simply means you're prioritizing your own growth and happiness.

Letting go doesn't always mean ending relationships entirely. Sometimes it's about creating boundaries—choosing how much time and energy you invest in certain connections. Boundaries are not walls; they're bridges to a healthier, more balanced version of your life. They allow you to protect your peace while still maintaining love and respect for others. This process can feel daunting, but it's also incredibly freeing. As you reflect on your relationships, ask yourself: *Who reminds me of my worth? Who pushes me to be my best self? And who makes me question my value or feel small?* The answers to these questions are your guideposts, helping you identify the connections that will propel you forward and the ones that may be holding you back.

And remember, this isn't about creating a perfect social circle or cutting ties with anyone who doesn't fit a certain mold. It's about aligning your relationships with your vision for the woman you're becoming. Sometimes, that means making changes—big or small—to ensure that the people in your life are helping you, not hindering you. You have the power to rewrite the script of your life. You are the one in control of who gets a starring role, who plays a supporting character, and who exits stage left. This is your story, and you deserve to surround yourself with people who make it richer, brighter, and more meaningful.

Take a moment to reflect. Who are the people who lift you up, who see your worth even when you don't? Who are the ones who make you feel alive, inspired, and capable? Hold onto those connections tightly. And for the relationships that feel like they're pulling you down, trust yourself to make the choices that will bring you closer to the life you want. Because at the end of the day, you are the director of this incredible movie called *you*.

One thing I want you to remember as you go through this:
You are not defined by any one moment or mistake.

This is a truth that's easier said than embraced, especially when life throws us challenges that shake the core of who we are. I learned this lesson the hard way, during a season of life when everything felt overwhelming, uncertain, and out of control.

When I received that bad performance review at work, I felt like the ground had been pulled out from under me. My initial reaction was anger. I convinced myself that I was being unfairly treated, that the timing was cruel and completely out of line. After all, I had spent nine months of the previous year pregnant, then took two months of maternity leave, navigating the most vulnerable and exhausting period of my life. On top of that, I had battled postpartum depression and severe anxiety. In my mind, the performance review felt like a personal attack—proof that my biggest fears about becoming a mother were coming true. For so long, I had worried that motherhood would somehow diminish my career, that stepping away even briefly would make me less valuable or less capable in the eyes of others. This review seemed to validate every insecurity I had buried deep inside. It wasn't just a critique of my work—it felt like a critique of *me*. In that moment, I wasn't just a woman trying to juggle the demands of life and motherhood; I was a failure. The more I thought about it, the more I leaned into the narrative of victimhood. *They don't understand how hard it is,* I told myself. *They're punishing me for being a mother.* I carried that weight with me, replaying the moment in my head, feeling anger and sadness swell with each repetition.

But then something shifted. In a rare moment of clarity—brought on by exhaustion from carrying that emotional burden—I decided to sit with the discomfort and really take inventory of what was happening. What was I feeling, and why? What was the truth of this situation? It wasn't easy, but I forced myself to confront the uncomfortable reality: *The problem wasn't them—it was me.* I had to be brutally honest with myself. Yes, the postpartum struggles were real. Yes, the transition into motherhood was one of the hardest things I'd ever done. But when it came to my work, I had to own my actions—or lack thereof. I had slacked off on calling clients, lost my sense of urgency, and failed to show up with the same commitment I once prided myself on. My boss wasn't out to get me. The review wasn't some malicious attempt to tear me down. It was a reflection of how I had been showing up—or not showing up—in my role.

Recognizing that truth was one of the most painful but freeing moments of my life. If I was the problem, that meant I also held the solution. I realized that I didn't have to let this one moment define me. I didn't have to carry the weight of shame or anger anymore. Instead, I could use it as a wake-up call, an opportunity to recalibrate and take control of my own story. From that point on, I started to show up differently—not just at work but in my life. I committed to being fully present to putting in the effort and focus that I knew I was capable of. Slowly, the pieces began to fall into place.

What I want you to take away from this is that your challenges, your mistakes, your hard moments—they don't define you. They are simply chapters in your story, not the entire narrative. Every decision, every step, every moment has brought you to this point, and each one holds the potential to teach you something valuable.

So, take some time today. Find a quiet space, take a deep breath, and get real with yourself. Acknowledge your strengths, your challenges, and your dreams. Look at your life with honesty but also with compassion. This isn't about beating yourself up or magnifying every misstep. It's about seeing your journey for what it is—a beautiful, messy, evolving story that has shaped the incredible woman you are today.

Be kind to yourself as you do this. You're doing the best you can with what you've got, and that's more than enough. Remember, this moment—whatever it looks like—is just one part of your journey. It's not the final word. You're on this path for a reason. Trust in that. Trust that every twist and turn has brought you closer to the woman you're becoming. And know this: The woman you are today has everything she needs to create the life you want. You are strong, you are capable, and you are worthy.

Grab your journal and reflect on these questions:

- What do I like about myself?

- What am I proud of?

- Where am I feeling out of alignment? Where am I feeling resistance in my life?

- Who is the woman I am today? What do I value? What matters most to me?

- Who lifts me up? Who are the main characters in my life?

- Who is holding me back?

- Where am I letting my past mistakes define who I am?

  Access the free workbook by scanning the QR code:

https://www.amandacahill.com/redefiningyouresources

Key Takeaways on Taking Inventory of the Woman You Are Today

- **You Are Evolving**: The woman you are today is a culmination of your experiences, choices, and lessons. Growth isn't a sign of failure—it's a natural part of your journey.

- **Self-Reflection Builds a Stronger Foundation**: Taking inventory of your strengths, values, and current state helps you understand who you are and where you want to grow. It's not about finding flaws but about celebrating how far you've come and identifying areas ready for change.

- **Self-Awareness Is an Act of Love**: Reflecting on who you are is not about judgment but about honoring your journey with compassion and curiosity. You're not looking for perfection—you're embracing your humanity.

- **Recognize and Celebrate Your Wins**: From small daily victories to life-changing accomplishments, acknowledging what makes you proud strengthens your self-belief and sets the stage for future growth.

- **Ask the Hard Questions**: Questions like "What do I like about myself?" and "Where am I feeling out of alignment?" provide clarity and help you identify areas where you can make meaningful shifts in your life.

- **Embrace Your Whole Self**: Confidence comes from accepting all parts of yourself—the strengths, the quirks, and even the perceived flaws. These make you beautifully human and uniquely you.

- **Reframe Mistakes as Growth Opportunities**: Challenges and setbacks don't define you. They are chapters in your story that offer valuable lessons and opportunities for self-awareness and change.

- **Align Your Relationships with Your Growth**: Surround yourself with people who lift you up and align with your vision for the future. Set boundaries or let go of relationships that drain your energy or hinder your progress.

- **Trust the Process**: Taking inventory of yourself is an ongoing journey. It's about acknowledging where you are, honoring your progress, and moving forward with intention and self-compassion.

- **You Are Enough**: The woman you are today is not a placeholder for your future self. She is worthy, capable, and extraordinary, just as she is, and she forms the foundation for everything you're building.

CHAPTER 6

Who Do You Want to Become?

"Create the highest, grandest vision possible for your life, because you become what you believe."
– Oprah Winfrey

Creating a vision for who you want to become is a transformative and deeply personal process. It's not just about setting goals or ticking off milestones—it's about painting a vivid, heart-centered picture of the life you truly desire and the woman you want to be at the center of it. Vision isn't just a plan; it's a lifeline that pulls you forward, helping you rise above the noise and chaos of the everyday. It's what keeps you grounded when everything around you feels uncertain.

Imagine waking up each morning feeling purposeful, not because your life is perfect but because it reflects what truly matters to you. Your days are filled with work that excites and fulfills you. The people around you lift you up, and the choices you make feel aligned with the life you've always dreamed of living. That's the power of an intentional life—the magic of stepping fully into the woman you've always wanted to become. It's not about chasing someone else's idea of happiness; it's about designing a life that feels authentic and joyful for you.

There was a time when envisioning the woman I wanted to become felt completely out of reach. I didn't even know where to start. Every day felt like a carbon copy of the one before it—wake up, rush through the motions, collapse into bed, and do it all over again. I felt lost in my own life, like I was going through the motions without any real sense of direction. It wasn't that I didn't care; it was that I didn't know how to change. Every moment felt like survival, not living. I didn't like the woman I was or how I was showing up in the world. I knew I wasn't bringing the best of myself to the people and things that mattered most. My relationships felt surface-level, my energy was drained, and my confidence was at an all-time low. I had this nagging sense that I was meant for more, but I couldn't see a way out of the rut I was in. It felt like I was stuck on a hamster wheel, running hard but getting nowhere.

One evening, after yet another exhausting day, I found myself sitting at my kitchen table with a journal in front of me. I stared at the blank page, unsure of what to write. I closed my eyes and took a deep breath, asking myself a simple but daunting question: *If I could create a life I truly loved, what would it look like?* At first, I didn't even know how to answer. The vision felt so far away, almost impossible. All I could see was the endless cycle I was trapped in. How could I dream about something better when I didn't even like where I was?

But slowly, as I allowed myself to sit with the question, something began to shift. I started to picture the woman I wanted to be—the woman I had forgotten somewhere along the way. She wasn't buried as deeply as I thought. I could see glimpses of her in the way I used to light up a room, in the dreams I once dared to have, in the parts of myself I had pushed aside for far too long. I imagined her waking up each morning with clarity and purpose, moving through her day with joy and strength. She had work that excited her, relationships that nurtured her, and a confidence that radiated from within. She wasn't perfect, but she was at peace with herself.

That vision became my compass. It gave me something to hold onto when my days still felt hard and repetitive. It reminded me that the woman I wanted to become wasn't some far-off stranger—she was already within me, waiting to be uncovered.

In this chapter, we'll explore how to create that vision for yourself. We'll delve into the qualities, values, and lifestyle that will shape the woman you want to be. This isn't just about dreaming big—it's about using that dream as a guide to shape your choices and actions today. Because here's the truth: You don't have to wait to become her. She's already a part of you, and every step you take brings her closer to the surface. It's time to stop surviving and start living intentionally. It's time to step into the woman you've always known you could be.

The Power of a Clear Destination

Think of your life like a GPS. Without a destination, the GPS will keep you moving, but you'll likely find yourself circling the same blocks, wasting time and energy, frustrated at the lack of progress. The same is true in life. Without a clear vision of where you're headed, it's easy to fall into routines that don't serve you, reacting to life rather than creating it. The GPS analogy perfectly captures how powerful and transformative it can be to set a destination for your life and the woman you want to become.

When you use a GPS, the first thing you do is input where you want to go. It doesn't ask you for every step you'll take or whether you know the exact path. It doesn't need to—it calculates the route for you. In the same way, having a vision for your life doesn't require you to know every twist and turn ahead. It simply requires you to know where you want to end up. Once you have that clarity, everything begins to align. The choices you make, the opportunities you notice, and the direction you take, all start to move you closer to your goal.

Life, like driving, is rarely a straight line. You'll encounter detours, traffic, and unexpected roadblocks. Maybe a relationship ends, a job doesn't pan out, or you face a personal challenge that slows you down. These moments can feel like setbacks, but just like a GPS recalculates when you take a wrong turn, your vision can adapt to these changes. The beauty of having a destination is that it keeps you moving forward, even if the route looks different than you originally planned. You're never truly lost as long as you know where you're going.

Another powerful aspect of the GPS analogy is that it allows for flexibility. Imagine setting out on a road trip with a specific destination in mind, but along the way, you discover new places you want to explore or decide to take a scenic route. Your GPS doesn't shut down because you've changed your mind. It recalculates, adjusting to your new preferences while keeping the destination in focus. The same applies to your life. Your vision isn't set in stone; it evolves as you do. The key is to stay connected to the essence of what you want and allow yourself the freedom to adjust as your goals and desires grow.

Now think about what happens when you don't set a destination at all. The GPS can't help you—it just shows you a blinking dot on a map, aimlessly moving with no direction. In life, this is how you end up feeling stuck or overwhelmed. You're busy, but nothing seems to be changing. The power of a clear destination is that it gives your actions purpose. Every choice you make becomes intentional and aligned with where you want to go, rather than just filling time.

Having a destination doesn't mean you'll never make mistakes or face challenges. It doesn't mean the road won't be bumpy or that you won't need to pause and rest along the way. What it does mean is that you'll always have a reason to keep going. You'll have something pulling you forward, something that excites and inspires you, even on the toughest days.

Take a moment to think about your own life. What is the destination you want to set in your GPS? What does your dream life look like? What kind of woman do you want to become? When you set that destination, you give yourself the gift of clarity. You might not know every step, but you'll know where you're headed. And that's what keeps you moving, growing, and becoming the person you're meant to be.

Living by Someone Else's Map

For too long, I found myself living by someone else's map. Like so many women, I had absorbed a set of expectations about what "success" should look like—expectations handed down by family, society, and well-meaning mentors. Stable career? Check. Financial security? Check. A home and family? Check. I had all the ingredients that were supposed to add up to a fulfilling life. But something was missing. Instead of feeling accomplished, I felt empty, like I was following a script someone else had written for me. Living by someone else's map is like driving with the wrong destination entered into your GPS. You can be moving forward, hitting all the milestones, but there's this nagging sense of disconnection. The turns you're taking don't feel right. You get to what should feel like your destination, and yet it doesn't feel like your place. That's exactly where I found myself. I wasn't chasing my definition of success; I was chasing what I thought I *should* want.

The problem with someone else's map is that it doesn't account for your heart, your passions, or your dreams. It leads to a life that looks good on the outside but feels off on the inside. For me, the wake-up call came when I realized I was exhausted from striving. I had built a life that checked all the socially approved boxes but left me asking, "Is this it? Is this all there is?" Every day began to feel like a grind, and I didn't recognize the woman I was becoming. That bright, happy woman who used to approach life with curiosity and energy was buried beneath layers of expectations and obligations.

Looking back, I realize that living by someone else's map is often unintentional. We absorb the ideas and beliefs of those around us, and without questioning them, we adopt them as our own. It's not that those expectations are bad or wrong—they're just not *yours*. They come from well-meaning parents, teachers, and friends who truly want what's best for you, but their vision of "best" is shaped by their experiences, not yours. It's a humbling realization to know you've been chasing goals that don't truly matter to you. But it's also an empowering one. Because the moment you acknowledge you're on the wrong path is the moment you can choose a different one. You don't have to keep driving toward a destination that doesn't feel right. You can pause, recalculate, and set a course that's aligned with who you are and what you really want.

The truth is, your map should reflect *your* dreams, not someone else's. It should lead you to a life that feels authentic and aligned, not one that simply looks good on paper. The beauty of life is that you get to rewrite your journey at any time. The moment you stop following someone else's map, you start creating a life that feels like home—a life that belongs wholly and completely to you.

The Fear of Dreaming Big

I'll admit, when I first started envisioning my ideal life, I was hesitant—almost paralyzed. The fear of dreaming big felt overwhelming, like standing at the edge of a cliff, unsure if I'd fly or fall. What if I set my sights too high and failed? What if I wasn't capable of reaching those dreams? These thoughts played on repeat in my mind, keeping me small and stuck in the comfort of mediocrity. It's not that I didn't have dreams—I just didn't think they were possible for me.

That fear of disappointment was so strong it felt safer not to dream at all. After all, if I didn't aim high, I couldn't fall short, right? But here's what I've learned: Your vision isn't about guarantees; it's about setting a direction. Like a GPS recalculates when you take a wrong turn, your vision can evolve, adapt, and guide you back to the path that feels right. The journey isn't linear, and it's not supposed to be. The key is to set a destination and start moving toward it, no matter how uncertain or imperfect the route might seem.

One of the biggest breakthroughs for me was shifting a single question in my mind. Instead of asking, "What if I fail?" I started asking, "What if I succeed?" This is just like we talked about in Chapter 3 in shifting the "what if" to success rather than failure. It sounds so simple, but that small change opened a door to possibilities I had never allowed myself to consider. Suddenly, the idea of failure wasn't the end—it was just part of the process. What if I could create a life that felt joyful, fulfilling, and aligned with my values? What if I succeeded in ways I couldn't even imagine yet?

That shift gave me permission to dream without limits. And here's what I realized: Dreaming big isn't about the outcome; it's about the growth that happens along the way. Every step you take toward your vision, no matter how small, is a victory. It's proof that you're capable of more than you think, that you have the courage to create a life that reflects who you truly are.

So, let yourself dream big. Give yourself permission to want more, even if it feels scary. Remember, the fear of dreaming big is just the echo of old doubts. You don't have to listen. Instead, lean into the excitement of possibility. Because the real question isn't "What if I fail?"—it's "What if I succeed beyond my wildest dreams?" And isn't that worth finding out?

Create a Vision for Your Future Self

You probably know exactly what you don't want in life. You don't want to feel stuck, unappreciated, or overwhelmed by the mundane. You don't want to be in toxic relationships or trapped in a job that drains your energy. But when someone asks you what you *do* want, do you hesitate? Do you find yourself struggling to articulate a clear vision of the life you desire and the woman you want to become? If you do, you're not alone—I've been there, too. As my dear friend and mentor Sarah

Centrella always says, "If you don't know what you want, how will you know if you've got it?" That truth is the crucial starting point for envisioning your future self. Without a clear vision, how will you ever recognize when you've arrived at the destination in your GPS for the life you've been dreaming of?

The beauty of creating a vision for your life is that it doesn't require you to know every single step you'll take to get there. It's not about having a foolproof roadmap; it's about setting a direction that excites you, inspires you, and pulls you toward the woman you're meant to become. This is where the incredible magic of your mind comes into play—specifically, the Reticular Activating System (RAS). Learning about the RAS through Ed Mylett's work completely transformed the way I understood my brain's ability to focus on what really matters.

Your RAS acts as a filter, sifting through the endless information your brain receives and directing your attention to what aligns with your current focus. For example, have you ever decided you want a specific car, only to suddenly start seeing it everywhere you go? The car didn't suddenly appear out of thin air; your RAS simply tuned in to notice it. It's the same reason why you can hear your name called across a crowded room—the RAS has been primed to prioritize that sound over all the others.

This concept applies directly to the vision you create for your future self. When you get crystal clear on what you want and who you want to become, your RAS starts working in the background, helping you notice opportunities, make connections, and align your actions with your goals. It's why crafting a vivid, detailed vision is so powerful—it literally trains your brain to help you achieve it.

So, how do you start creating this vision? First, let's shift your focus from what you don't want to what you truly desire. Take a moment to reflect on what you want your future to hold. Who are you in this vision?

Picture yourself at your happiest and most fulfilled. What kind of work are you doing? Is it something that lights you up and makes you feel alive? Imagine your ideal day—how do you start your mornings? How do your evenings wind down? Who is by your side, celebrating and supporting you along the way? What does your dream life feel like? When you envision your future self, who is she? What qualities does she embody? This isn't about indulging in idle daydreams—it's about painting a vivid, inspiring picture of the woman you are becoming. See her. Feel her strength, her confidence, and her joy. Notice how she moves through the world, how she treats others, and how she carries herself. When you can see this woman clearly, something powerful begins to happen. You start to embody her qualities in your daily life. You begin to move like her, think like her, and make decisions that align with the life she's living.

The process of creating this vision is both an art and a science. It requires you to tune out the noise of others' expectations and tune into the quiet whispers of your own desires. It takes courage to imagine a life that feels extraordinary, especially if it looks nothing like the life you're living now. But that's the point. Vision isn't about staying within the boundaries of what feels safe or familiar. It's about daring to dream of something greater and believing in the possibility of more.

Keep in mind: Vague desires lead to vague outcomes. That's why it's so important to be specific about your vision. Don't just say, "I want to be happy." Define what happiness looks like for you. Is it waking up without an alarm clock, energized and ready to take on the day? Is it having the freedom to travel, spending quality time with loved ones, or pursuing your passions with joy and enthusiasm? Is it knowing that the work you do makes a meaningful difference in the world? The more detailed you can be, the more your RAS can help you recognize and pursue the opportunities that align with your goals. And remember, your vision isn't a fixed destination. Just like a GPS recalculates when you take a different route, your vision can evolve as you do. As you grow and change, your desires may shift—and that's okay. The important part is to keep checking in with yourself to make sure the life you're building still aligns with the woman you're becoming.

Creating a vision for your future self isn't just about the destination; it's about the transformation that happens along the way. It's about becoming the woman you've always dreamed of being and stepping into a life that feels deeply fulfilling, joyful, and true to who you are. You have everything you need within you to make this vision a reality. Now it's time to set the destination and begin the journey.

Let's take a moment to pause and reflect. Close your eyes and imagine your future self. Picture her clearly. Where is she? What is she doing? Who is by her side? What does her life feel like? Hold onto that image. That's your destination. It's the life you're working toward. And just like a GPS, there will be many routes to get there. Some may be quicker, others more scenic. You may face detours or obstacles along the way, but as long as you know where you're going and stay focused on your vision, you'll keep moving forward. Now, open your eyes and write down what you envisioned following these prompts:

1. **Define Your Values:** Start by identifying the core values that matter most to you. These could include qualities like integrity, kindness, growth, resilience, or adventure. Ask yourself, *What values do I want to live by?* Defining these values will help you create a vision that feels meaningful and true to you.

2. **Imagine Your Ideal Day:** Picture a day in the life of the woman you want to become. What does her morning routine look like? How does she spend her time? Who does she surround herself with? This exercise helps bring your vision to life, giving it shape and substance beyond just abstract ideas.

3. **Visualize Key Areas of Life:** Think about the main areas of life—career, relationships, health, finances, and hobbies. Write down what you envision in each of these areas for your future self. Be specific and detailed, describing how you want to feel and what you want to experience.

4. **Set Aspirational Qualities:** Consider the qualities and strengths that you admire in others and want to cultivate in yourself. This might include confidence, resilience, patience, or creativity. Write down these aspirational qualities as part of your vision, knowing that you're capable of growing into them over time.

Bridge the Gap Between Now and the Future

Once you have a clear vision, the next step is to start bridging the gap between who you are today and who you want to become. This doesn't happen overnight; it's a gradual process of making intentional choices that align with your vision. Each small action brings you closer to that future self.

For me, bridging this gap involved defining goals and re-evaluating my daily habits and routines. I began asking myself, *Is this choice helping me become the woman I want to be?* Whether it was choosing to exercise, setting boundaries, or investing time in personal growth, each decision felt like a step toward my ideal life. Over time, these small, intentional actions created momentum, and I could feel myself evolving into the woman I envisioned. Some days will feel like leaps forward, while others may feel like small steps. Both are valuable. The journey of becoming your future self is less about perfection and more about persistence. With each step, you're not only creating a life that aligns with your vision but also building a foundation of self-trust and confidence. In the next few chapters, I'll show you my process for taking the vision you've created and putting real, actionable steps to help bring that vision to life.

Grab your journal and reflect on these questions:

- When I think about my future self,

  o Who am I? What characteristics do I embody? How would others describe me?

  o What values do I want to live by?

  o What do I look like?

  o What am I doing for work (do I work at all)?

  o How do I treat others?

  o How do my days begin and end? (What am I doing to start and end my day?)

  o Who is by my side, supporting and celebrating me?

  o What does my dream life feel like?

  o What does success mean to me?

  o What makes me happy?

  Access the free workbook by scanning the QR code:

https://www.amandacahill.com/redefiningyouresources

Key Takeaways on Envisioning the Woman You Want to Become

- **Vision as Your Compass**: Envisioning your future self provides clarity and direction. Like setting a destination in a GPS, your vision helps you navigate life's twists and turns, keeping you grounded and motivated, even when the path gets challenging.

- **Authenticity Over Expectations**: The life you create should reflect your own values, dreams, and desires—not society's expectations or someone else's definition of success. Living intentionally starts with creating a map that's uniquely yours.

- **The Power of "What If"**: Fear of failure often holds us back from dreaming big. Shifting your mindset from "What if I fail?" to "What if I succeed?" opens up endless possibilities and encourages you to pursue your vision with courage and hope.

- **Your Vision Activates Change**: When you create a vivid, detailed picture of your future self, your Reticular Activating System (RAS) helps align your thoughts, actions, and opportunities with that vision, propelling you toward your goals.

- **Define What You Want**: Knowing what you want—not just what you don't want—is crucial. Be specific about your values, daily routines, relationships, career aspirations, and the qualities you want to embody to create a meaningful, actionable vision.

- **Growth Through Action**: Bridging the gap between your current self and your future self requires consistent, intentional actions. Small, daily steps aligned with your vision create momentum and help you embody the woman you want to become.

- **Dream Without Limits**: Your vision doesn't have to fit within the boundaries of your current reality. Allow yourself to dream big, knowing that your future self is already within you, waiting to emerge through your efforts and belief.

- **Flexibility Is Key**: Life will bring detours and changes, but your vision can adapt and evolve. Stay connected to your core desires while allowing your path to shift as you grow and learn.

- **Use Prompts to Clarify Your Vision**: Reflect on questions like:

  o What are my core values?

  o What does my ideal day look like?

  o What do I want in key areas of life (career, relationships, health, finances, hobbies)?

  o What qualities do I aspire to embody?

- **Embrace the Journey**: Becoming the woman you want to be is a process. Each choice you make today is a step toward that vision. Celebrate your progress, knowing that both big leaps and small steps are meaningful.

CHAPTER 7

Embrace Your Future Self

"The future belongs to those who believe in the beauty of their dreams." – Eleanor Roosevelt

Transformation begins with a shift in identity. To truly embrace the future self you've envisioned, you must see her not as a distant ideal but as someone you are capable of becoming today. The life you've dreamed of isn't waiting for the "perfect moment" or a magical day when everything aligns—it's waiting for you to take that first step.

Think of the GPS analogy we've discussed. The moment you input a destination, it doesn't just sit idle and wait for you to arrive. It guides you, step by step, recalibrating when you take a wrong turn and helping you find the best path forward. But here's the thing: the GPS only works when you've set a clear destination. This is where the identity shift comes in. You're not just pointing yourself in the right direction— you're stepping into the mindset of the woman who is already on her way.

The Power of Identity Shifts

One of the most transformative aspects of stepping into your future self is the shift in identity that takes place. When you start to see yourself differently, your actions naturally begin to align with that new identity. You're no longer waiting for change to happen; you're creating it by embodying the qualities, values, and mindset of your future self.

Identity shifts are powerful because they affect everything from your habits to your relationships and your approach to challenges. For example, if your vision includes becoming a confident, empowered leader, begin by identifying the qualities of that future self: courage, resilience, and self-assurance. Then, ask yourself, *How would a confident leader approach this situation?* By viewing each decision through the lens of your future self, you're rewiring your mind to think, feel, and act in alignment with that identity.

For me, this became painfully clear when I decided to embrace a new identity as a "fit, happy, healthy mom." I remember sitting on the couch, exhausted and feeling far from the version of myself I wanted to be. I was out of shape, my energy levels were low, and my happiness felt buried under layers of self-doubt. But as I looked at my son playing nearby, I realized that my vision for the future wasn't just about me—it was about him, too. I wanted to be the kind of mom who could run around the park, who had the energy to play and the confidence to model a healthy, happy lifestyle. The problem was, I didn't see myself as that mom—not yet. I saw someone who was stuck, someone who didn't quite know how to begin. And that's when I realized that the shift had to start in my mind before it could take root in my life. I couldn't wait to feel like a "fit, happy, healthy mom" to act like one. I had to start acting as if I already was her.

The first step I took was simple but intentional: I began adding reminders about my goals to my calendar at random times throughout the year. These reminders would pop up unexpectedly—a quick nudge that said, "How's it going, future self?" or "Are you showing up as the mom you want to be today?" I'll share more on this in a minute. These small prompts became lifelines during moments of doubt or distraction, pulling me back on track and reminding me of the commitment I had made to myself and my son.

At first, the actions I took felt small and almost insignificant. I swapped one unhealthy snack for a healthier option. I took a short walk, even when I didn't feel like it. I started saying affirmations to myself in the mirror: "I am becoming the fit, happy, healthy mom I envision." Each action felt awkward at first, like trying on an identity that didn't quite fit. But over time, those small, intentional choices began to add up. The more I acted like the woman I wanted to become, the more I started to see her in myself.

What I learned is this: Embracing your future self isn't about perfection—it's about progress. It's about making decisions today that align with the person you're becoming, even when it feels uncomfortable or unnatural. It's about reminding yourself, daily, that the woman you want to be is already within you, waiting for you to step into her shoes.

This process isn't linear. There were days when I doubted myself, days when I felt like giving up. But I kept going because I had a clear destination and a reason bigger than myself. My son became my why— my anchor in moments of uncertainty. Every time I thought about giving up, I reminded myself of the mom I wanted to be for him. And with every step I took, I began to see that version of myself more clearly.

As you move forward on your journey, remember that transformation starts with a single decision. It starts with choosing to believe in the woman you're becoming, even before you see evidence of her in your life. It starts with aligning your thoughts, actions, and choices with the vision you've created, trusting that each small step will lead you closer to the life you desire.

The journey to your future self won't always be easy, but it will be worth it. Every action you take, no matter how small, is a vote for the person you're becoming. And every time you choose to embrace that identity— whether it's through a decision to move your body, a reminder that pops up on your calendar, or a quiet moment of self-reflection—you're building the foundation for a life that feels authentic, fulfilling, and uniquely yours.

Acting "As If"

Transformation doesn't happen in the distant future—it begins now, in the small, intentional ways you show up every day. Acting "as if" is the bridge between who you are today and the woman you are becoming. It's about aligning your actions with the identity you're stepping into, reinforcing the mindset and habits that will shape your future self.

When I decided to become a fit, happy, healthy mom, the gap between where I was and where I wanted to be felt enormous. I was tired, out of shape, and overwhelmed. I didn't feel like a vibrant, healthy mom—I felt like I was barely surviving. But I knew the woman I wanted to be, and I committed to acting as if I was already her. It wasn't about pretending; it was about embodying the small, consistent actions that would move me closer to that version of myself.

Every morning, I'd ask myself, *What would a fit, happy, healthy mom do today?* The answer wasn't complicated: She would prioritize her health and well-being. So, I started with what I could manage. I took short walks in the mornings, imagining the version of me who walked confidently, feeling energized and strong. I didn't feel like that woman yet, but each walk was a vote for her, a small step in her direction. I also made small adjustments to my daily routine—packing healthier lunches, drinking more water, and finding joy in simple moments with my husband and son. Over time, these changes began to add up. I started to see myself differently, not just as someone trying to get fit, but as someone who was becoming that vibrant, healthy mom. The more I acted in alignment with this new identity, the easier it became to make choices that supported it.

One strategy that helped me stay on track was building reminders into my calendar. These reminders weren't about pressure; they were about encouragement. They'd pop up at random times, saying things like,

"You are becoming the healthy, happy mom you envisioned" or "Check in: Are your actions today aligned with your goals?" On tough days, these reminders served as a lifeline, bringing me back to my "why" and keeping me grounded in my vision. This process isn't about achieving perfection. It's about progress. Acting "as if" doesn't mean you won't face setbacks or moments of doubt—it means you keep showing up anyway. It's about asking yourself, *What's one thing I can do today to move closer to my future self?* and then doing it, no matter how small.

When I reflect on this journey, I realize that acting "as if" wasn't just a tool for achieving goals; it was a practice that redefined how I saw myself. With each small action, I was rewriting my story, turning a vision into reality. And that's the power of this practice—it's not about waiting for the perfect moment or feeling like you've already arrived. It's about showing up as the woman you want to be and trusting that every small step matters.

So, what does this look like for you? What's one thing your future self would do today? Maybe it's taking a walk, speaking up in a meeting, or carving out time for something that lights you up. Whatever it is, remember: each action is a vote for your future self. And with every vote, you're not just imagining her—you're becoming her.

Visualize Your Future Self Daily

Visualization is a powerful tool for transformation. By taking just a few moments each day to imagine the woman you want to become, you're planting seeds of change in your mind and reinforcing your commitment to your goals. This isn't just daydreaming—it's a deliberate practice that helps you internalize your new identity and align your actions with your vision.

Start by finding a quiet space where you won't be disturbed. Close your eyes and take a few deep breaths. Now, picture your future self. See her clearly in your mind's eye. How does she carry herself? How does she feel? Imagine her walking through her day with confidence, making choices that reflect her values and goals. Visualize her as if she's already real because, in a way, she is.

When I began the journey of becoming a fit, happy, healthy mom, visualization was what kept me grounded and focused. In the beginning, it felt impossible to see myself as that woman. I didn't feel healthy or happy, and the version of me that I wanted to become seemed so far away. But I knew that if I couldn't see her in my mind, I'd never become her in reality. Every morning, before the chaos of the day began, I sat down and closed my eyes. I visualized myself as that mom—energetic, vibrant, and fully present for my son. I pictured myself running alongside him at the park, feeling strong and alive. I imagined mornings when I woke up excited and ready to take on the day, fueling my body with nourishing food and moving in ways that made me feel good. I saw myself smiling, confident in my body, and deeply connected to my role as both a mother and a woman who took care of herself. At first, it felt awkward, even forced. My mind wanted to return to the version of me that felt stuck—tired, overwhelmed, and out of shape. But I kept coming back to that vision, allowing it to guide me. I focused on how she felt in those moments: light, joyful, and empowered. Those feelings became my motivation, reminding me of why I wanted this transformation.

Over time, this practice began to shift how I saw myself. I started to believe in that future version of me. I wasn't just hoping to become her; I began acting as if I already was her. I started making small, intentional choices—choosing a walk over another episode of TV, prepping meals that made me feel energized, and carving out time to play with my son instead of scrolling through my phone. These small steps built momentum, and before I knew it, I began to feel like the woman I had been visualizing.

Visualization is about more than seeing your future self; it's about connecting with her emotionally. Feel her joy, her confidence, and her strength. By anchoring yourself in those emotions, you teach your mind to believe that this version of you is possible. And the more you practice, the more natural it becomes to make choices that align with her.

To make visualization a consistent habit, tie it to an existing routine— whether it's during your morning coffee, while brushing your teeth, or before bed. These moments of stillness create space for you to reconnect with the vision of your future self, ensuring that she stays at the forefront of your mind.

For me, visualizing the fit, happy, healthy mom I wanted to become wasn't just a tool—it was a lifeline. It reminded me every day that transformation starts in the mind. The more I saw her, the more I became her, and that realization changed everything. Let this practice serve as your daily reminder that you are capable of stepping into the life you've envisioned, one thought, one action, and one day at a time.

Challenge Old Beliefs

Stepping into your future self is an act of courage, one that requires you to confront the beliefs that have kept you tethered to the past. Just as we discussed in Chapter 3, as we redefined your beliefs, these old, limiting beliefs often resurface as you move closer to the woman you want to become. They whisper doubts and insecurities, urging you to stay comfortable in the familiar. But here's the truth: Growth doesn't happen in comfort zones. If a belief no longer serves the future you're striving toward, it's time to challenge it and rewrite the narrative.

When I started my journey to becoming a fit, happy, healthy mom, I wasn't just facing physical hurdles—I was wrestling with a mountain of deeply ingrained beliefs. Two of the loudest voices in my head were painfully familiar: "Getting in shape and being thin is hard," and "I'm always tired and exhausted, and that will never change." These beliefs weren't fleeting thoughts; they felt like truths etched into my identity, reinforced by years of feeling stuck and overwhelmed. The belief that "getting in shape and being thin is hard" stemmed from years of failed attempts to prioritize my health. I had tried diets, workout plans, and routines that never stuck. Each time I gave up, it added another layer to the story that I wasn't someone who could succeed in this area. Pair that with "I'm always tired and exhausted, and that will never change," and it felt like I was trapped in a cycle that was impossible to break. With a demanding schedule and the relentless exhaustion of motherhood, how could I ever hope to be the energetic, vibrant mom I envisioned?

But beliefs are not facts. They're stories we've told ourselves over time, often based on past experiences or societal conditioning. And like any story, they can be rewritten.

I remember a specific moment that shifted everything. It was a Saturday morning, and I caught myself repeating the same mantra of frustration in my mind: *I'm too tired for this.* I looked at my son, running around with boundless energy, and I realized how much I wanted to match his enthusiasm—to feel strong enough to chase him, to play freely without feeling drained. That realization was the spark I needed. If my belief was keeping me stuck, it was time to challenge it.

I started asking myself a critical question: *Is this belief serving the woman I want to become?* The answer was a resounding no. From that moment, I made a conscious decision to rewrite those stories. "Getting in shape and being thin is hard" became "Taking care of my body is how I honor myself and my family." "I'm always tired and exhausted, and that will never change" became "Prioritizing my energy and health will help me show up as the mom I want to be."

The process wasn't instant or easy. Each time those limiting beliefs crept back in, I had to actively replace them with my new, empowering narratives. When I felt like skipping a workout, I reminded myself that movement was a gift, not a chore. When I wanted to reach for an unhealthy snack out of exhaustion, I paused and asked, *What would the fit, happy, healthy mom choose right now?*

What I discovered along the way was that challenging my beliefs wasn't just about changing my mindset—it was about changing my identity. I stopped seeing myself as someone who was tired and stuck and started seeing myself as a woman who was actively creating the life she wanted. Each small decision reinforced that new identity and made it easier to keep going.

As you step into your future self, take a moment to identify the beliefs that might be holding you back. Write them down, and ask yourself, *Is this belief serving my future self?* If it's not, replace it with one that does. Then, commit to living that new belief every day. Remember, your beliefs are the foundation for your actions, and your actions shape your reality. Transformation isn't just about changing what you do; it's about challenging and reshaping what you believe. When you let go of the stories that no longer serve you, you create space for a new narrative— one that aligns with the vibrant, empowered woman you're becoming. Each time you challenge an old belief, you're stepping closer to the life you've envisioned, and you're proving to yourself that change is not only possible—it's already happening.

Make Decisions as Your Future Self

Every decision you make is a building block of the person you're becoming. When faced with choices, big or small, consider this question: "What would my future self do?" This simple yet powerful practice acts as a compass, keeping you aligned with the vision of who you want to become.

When I was on my journey to becoming a fit, happy, healthy mom, I faced countless moments of decision-making that could either push me closer to that vision or pull me further away. Some of these choices seemed small—like whether to prepare a healthy lunch or grab fast food—but in those moments, they felt monumental. I would pause and ask myself, *What would the fit, happy, healthy mom do?* The answer was clear. She would fuel her body with food that gave her the energy to keep up with her toddler. She would prioritize her well-being because she knew it allowed her to show up as her best self for her family.

There were also harder decisions. I had to choose whether to prioritize sleep over staying up late to scroll social media or binge-watch shows. I had to decide if I was going to let a long day at work derail my plans to move my body or if I'd find 20 minutes to do something active, even if it wasn't perfect. I began to see every decision as an opportunity to step into the identity of my future self. Over time, these small but intentional decisions built the habits and mindset that transformed me into the woman I envisioned.

This practice isn't about being perfect; it's about being intentional. Maybe your vision is to become a confident leader at work. When you're faced with a challenging conversation, ask yourself, *What would a confident leader do?* Would she avoid the situation or address it head-on with grace and clarity? If your future self is someone who prioritizes self-care, ask, *Would she say yes to this extra commitment, or would she honor her need for rest?*

Making decisions as your future self takes practice. At first, it might feel unnatural, especially if you're used to operating on autopilot or making choices based on old habits. But the more you do it, the more natural it becomes. You start to notice how these decisions compound over time, creating momentum toward the life you're designing.

Here's the beauty of this approach: It empowers you to live in alignment with your goals even before you fully achieve them. Each decision, no matter how small, is a declaration of who you are becoming. It's a signal to yourself and the world that you are serious about your transformation. Over time, these choices become second nature, and the gap between your current self and your future self begins to close. You're no longer just dreaming of the woman you want to be—you're living as her, one decision at a time.

Living with Purpose and Intention

As you step into your future self, remember this important truth: Transformation isn't about becoming someone entirely new; it's about peeling back the layers of doubt, fear, and expectations to reveal the woman you've always been. Living with purpose and intention means committing to your vision every single day, even when progress feels slow, or life throws unexpected challenges your way. It's about aligning your actions with your values, showing up authentically, and honoring your unique journey.

When I began my transformation into the fit, happy, healthy mom I wanted to be, it felt like I was climbing a mountain that had no clear summit. The path wasn't always straight, and there were plenty of detours along the way. But I learned that every step mattered. Some days, progress was as simple as choosing to drink more water or taking a walk outside. Other days, it meant confronting the beliefs and habits that no longer served me. Each choice, no matter how small, was a declaration of my commitment to my vision.

The same is true for you. Living with purpose and intention doesn't mean every day will feel like a giant leap forward. It means learning to celebrate the small victories and embracing the setbacks as part of your growth. Each moment of alignment with your vision, whether it's choosing rest when you need it, showing up fully for your loved ones, or tackling a challenge with courage, is a step closer to becoming the woman you've envisioned.

This journey requires self-compassion. There will be days when you doubt yourself, when old habits resurface, or when you feel like giving up. In those moments, remind yourself that transformation is not about perfection—it's about persistence. Living with intention means allowing yourself grace and continuing forward, knowing that the path to your future self is rarely linear but always worth it.

One of the most powerful shifts I experienced on this journey was learning to trust the process. Instead of focusing solely on the end goal, I began to appreciate the growth and lessons along the way. Every challenge I faced, every choice I made, shaped me into the woman I wanted to become. Living with intention meant letting go of the need to control every outcome and embracing the beauty of the journey itself.

As you close this chapter, take a moment to reflect on the woman you are becoming. She's already within you, waiting to be fully realized. Each time you align your actions with your values and dreams, you're embodying her more and more. Transformation isn't something that happens in the distant future—it's happening now, with every intentional step you take.

So, keep going. Keep making choices that reflect the life you want to live and the woman you want to be. Trust in your ability to grow, evolve, and create a life that feels purposeful and authentic. You have the power to embrace your future self, and with every decision, you're proving that you are capable of becoming her. This isn't just your journey of transformation—it's your journey home to yourself.

Grab your journal and reflect on these questions:

- Where can you tie visualization into an already existing habit or part of your routine?

- How does your future self navigate her day-to-day life?

- What old beliefs or self-doubts are holding you back from fully embracing your future self?

- What small, intentional actions can you take today to begin living as your future self?

- How can you use the "acting as if" strategy in your daily life?

- What systems or tools can you implement to stay on track with your transformation?

- What is your "why" for embracing your future self, and how can you stay connected to it?

Access the free workbook by scanning the QR code:

https://www.amandacahill.com/redefiningyouresources

Key Takeaways on Embracing Your Future Self

- **Identity Shifts Drive Transformation**: To become your future self, you must shift your mindset and identity to align with her qualities, values, and habits. Ask yourself how she would handle situations and begin acting "as if" you are already her.

- **Start with Small Actions**: Transformation happens one step at a time. Every intentional choice, no matter how small, is a vote for your future self. These small, consistent actions build momentum and help align your present reality with your vision.

- **Act "As If" Today**: Acting "as if" bridges the gap between who you are now and who you want to be. Make decisions and take actions that reflect the qualities of your future self, even if they feel awkward or unnatural at first.

- **Visualization as a Tool for Change**: Daily visualization strengthens your belief in your future self and keeps your vision top of mind. Picture her clearly—how she moves, feels, and lives—and let that vision guide your actions.

- **Challenge Limiting Beliefs**: Old beliefs often hold us back from stepping into the next version of ourselves. Identify and rewrite these beliefs, replacing them with empowering narratives that align with your future self.

- **Make Decisions with Purpose**: Use the question "What would my future self do?" as a compass for decision-making. This practice aligns your choices with your long-term goals and builds confidence in your ability to create meaningful change.

- **Live with Intention**: Progress isn't always about giant leaps— it's about consistent, intentional steps. Celebrate small victories and embrace setbacks as opportunities for growth. Trust the process and stay connected to your vision.

- **Transformation Is Already Happening**: Your future self isn't a distant stranger; she's already within you, emerging through your actions and mindset shifts. Every intentional choice brings you closer to her.

- **Focus on Progress, Not Perfection**: The journey toward your future self isn't linear, and perfection isn't required. What matters is persistence and the daily commitment to align your actions with your vision.

- **Trust the Journey**: Transformation is about more than reaching an end goal—it's about appreciating the growth and lessons along the way. With each step, you're not just creating the life you want; you're uncovering the woman you've always been meant to be.

SECTION 3:

HABITS FOR LASTING CHANGE

CHAPTER 8

Vision-Aligned Goals

"Envision the woman you want to become, and then start showing up as her—one decision, one habit, one step at a time." – Unknown

With a clear vision of the woman you want to become, the next step is to set goals that bring that vision to life. Vision-aligned goals aren't just about checking off boxes or reaching milestones; they're about intentionally crafting a life that feels meaningful and true to who you are. These goals are designed to guide you step by step toward the future you've envisioned, creating a bridge between where you are now and where you want to be.

In my own journey, I discovered how unfulfilling it could be to set goals without a clear vision. I would strive, work hard, and even achieve what I set out to do, but something was always missing. The wins felt hollow, and instead of the pride or joy I thought I'd feel, I was left wondering, *Is this it?* It wasn't until I started aligning my goals with my vision for the future that everything shifted. Suddenly, my goals had purpose. They weren't just tasks on a to-do list; they were stepping stones leading me closer to the woman I wanted to become. Each goal, no matter how small, was infused with meaning because it was part of a bigger picture— my picture.

This chapter is about helping you do the same. Together, we'll explore how to set goals that reflect your core values, align with your vision, and move you forward with clarity and intention. By the end, you'll understand how to turn your dreams into actionable steps and create a life that feels truly aligned with who you are and where you're going.

The Importance of Goal Alignment

When we set goals that align with our vision, something powerful happens. These goals aren't just tasks to complete; they become a reflection of our deepest values and the future we aspire to create. They resonate on a personal level, which makes us more motivated and committed to achieving them. Think about it—when a goal truly matters to you, you're willing to push through obstacles, stay focused during challenges, and keep moving forward, even when the journey gets tough. That's the power of alignment.

Goals that connect to your vision hold a deeper meaning. They aren't just about checking off boxes or meeting arbitrary standards; they represent milestones on your path to becoming your ideal self. Each step brings you closer to the person you're striving to be, which adds purpose to the process. Whether it's choosing to work on your health, foster meaningful relationships, or build a career you're passionate about, these goals aren't isolated efforts—they're part of a larger story, your story.

Aligning your goals with your vision also frees you from the trap of living for others' expectations. It's easy to chase goals based on societal pressures or what others believe you *should* want. Maybe it's the "perfect" job, a milestone you're told is essential, or even a lifestyle that looks good on paper but doesn't feel right in your heart. True fulfillment comes from achieving goals that matter to *you*. By focusing on vision-aligned goals, you're honoring your own path and creating a life that feels authentic, rewarding, and uniquely yours.

From Vision to Action

A clear vision is your destination, but goals are the stepping stones that get you there. Think of your vision as a beautiful, inspiring picture of your future—the kind that excites you and fills you with purpose. But without actionable goals to guide you, even the most compelling vision can feel overwhelming or unattainable. Goals act as the bridge between where you are now and the future you're working to create. They break your vision into achievable steps and give you a roadmap for making it a reality.

The key to effective goal-setting is intentionality. Your goals should reflect your vision, align with your values, and be specific enough to keep you on track. For example, if your vision includes becoming healthier and more energetic, your goals might involve regular exercise, meal planning, or improving your sleep habits. These aren't just random tasks—they're aligned with your overall vision, making them more meaningful and motivating.

Clarity is also essential. Vague goals like "I want to be successful" or "I want to feel happier" are hard to act on because they lack direction. Instead, focus on creating goals that are specific, measurable, and actionable. For example, "I want to wake up feeling energized" could translate into a goal of going to bed by 10 p.m. every night.

Finally, remember that progress is made through consistent, manageable steps. Breaking your goals into smaller milestones not only makes them more achievable but also keeps you motivated by allowing you to celebrate along the way. With vision-aligned goals, you're not just checking boxes—you're intentionally building the life you've always imagined.

When I reflect on the process of writing this book, I realize how much this concept of vision-aligned goals was the foundation of bringing it to life. The moment I signed the contract with my publisher, I knew I was stepping into a new chapter—not just as a writer but as the woman I envisioned becoming. Writing this book wasn't just a professional milestone; it was a deeply personal journey of aligning my actions with the vision I had created for myself.

From the start, I knew this wasn't going to be easy. The idea of completing an entire manuscript was daunting, and doubt crept in more than once. Could I do this? Was I really the woman who could write a book that would inspire others? I quickly realized that the only way to overcome those fears was to break the overwhelming task into smaller, actionable goals that aligned with my vision. The vision I had for myself—a woman who leads with authenticity, empowers others, and shares her story to inspire transformation—became my guiding light. Each time doubt threatened to take over, I returned to that vision and reminded myself why this book mattered. Then, I turned that vision into action.

The first step was creating a clear roadmap. I broke the project into manageable phases: brainstorming, outlining, drafting, revising, and finalizing. Each phase had its own set of goals, and I gave myself realistic deadlines to stay on track. For example, I set a goal to complete the book outline within the first month. It was a small, achievable step, but crossing it off my list gave me a surge of confidence that fueled my progress.

I also committed to weekly writing goals. Instead of focusing on the enormity of the entire manuscript, I aimed to write a certain number of words each week. Some weeks, it was 2,000 words; other weeks, it was just 500. The key was consistency. Even on days when the words didn't flow easily, I showed up, reminding myself that progress—not perfection—was what mattered.

To stay aligned with my vision, I also made a point to celebrate the small wins along the way. Completing a chapter, receiving feedback from my editor, or even just hitting my word count for the week became moments of celebration. These milestones reminded me that each step was bringing me closer to the woman I was becoming and the impact I hoped this book would have.

But it wasn't just about the tactical goals. Writing this book required me to be intentional about my mindset and habits. I prioritized self-care—knowing that to pour my heart into these pages, I needed to be mentally and emotionally grounded. I set boundaries with my time, carving out dedicated writing sessions and saying no to distractions that didn't align with my priorities. I leaned on my support system, from my husband to my closest friends, who encouraged me every step of the way.

There were moments of doubt, of course—times when the task felt too big or when I questioned whether my words would resonate. But each time, I reminded myself of the vision: a woman who not only dreamed of writing a book but actually did it. A woman who turned her story into a tool for helping others redefine their own lives. That vision was my anchor, and my goals were the stepping stones that kept me moving forward.

Looking back, I see how every small action added up to something greater. What started as a daunting idea became a tangible reality because I aligned my goals with my vision and took it one step at a time. This book exists because of that commitment—because I chose to trust the process, honor the vision, and take action even when it felt uncomfortable.

That's the power of vision-aligned goals. They transform abstract dreams into achievable steps, giving you the momentum to move forward with purpose. Whether your vision is to write a book, start a new career, or simply feel more fulfilled in your daily life, the path forward starts with intentional, actionable goals. By staying true to your vision and breaking it into manageable steps, you'll find that the seemingly impossible becomes not only possible but deeply rewarding.

And here's the best part: every goal you achieve, no matter how small, brings you closer to the life you've envisioned—and to the woman you're becoming.

Steps for Setting Vision-Aligned Goals

1. **Define Your "Why":** Defining your "why" is the anchor that keeps you grounded when the process gets tough or the path forward feels unclear. It's not just about what you're doing; it's about why you're doing it. For me, the decision to write this book wasn't just about putting words on a page—it was about creating something that aligned with the vision I had for my life and the impact I wanted to make. My "why" was deeply personal: I wanted to share a message of transformation, resilience, and empowerment with women who, like me, have felt lost or stretched too thin.

    When the challenges of writing emerged—writer's block, self-doubt, or the pressure of deadlines—my "why" kept me going. I reminded myself that this book wasn't just a project; it was a reflection of the woman I was becoming. Each word was a step toward realizing my vision of helping others redefine themselves, just as I had.

    Your "why" works the same way. It's the emotional connection that breathes life into your goals and fuels your perseverance. Whether your goal is to write a book, start a business, or improve your health, ask yourself: What does this represent for my future self? Why does it matter? When your goals are rooted in a clear, meaningful purpose, you'll find the motivation to show up, even on the hardest days.

2. **Be Specific and Clear:** Vague goals lead to vague results. Instead of saying, "I want to be healthier," define what that means for you. What does healthier look like? How do you measure it? Is it a specific pant size or body fat percentage? Does it look like exercising three times a week? Cooking dinner at home five days a week? Drinking a specific number of glasses of water a day? The clearer you are about what you want to achieve, the easier it will be to measure

your progress and stay on track. This is also how your RAS will be able to help you achieve the goal. Your brain needs specificity to process what you really want and start to find ways to bring it into your life.

For example:

Vision: "I want to feel strong and energized in my body."

Goal: "I will work out 3 times a week for 30 minutes, focusing on strength training and cardio."

This specificity turns an abstract desire into something concrete and achievable.

Vision: "I want to become more confident and assertive in my professional life."

Goal: "I will speak up in at least one meeting each week, sharing a clear idea or suggestion, and prepare talking points beforehand to feel more confident."

This specific goal helps build confidence gradually while providing actionable steps to practice assertiveness in a professional setting.

Vision: "I want to create more balance in my life and feel present with my family."

Goal: "I will dedicate two weeknights as 'no-work zones' to spend uninterrupted time with my family, engaging in activities like dinner together or a game night."

This goal prioritizes family time, creating clear boundaries that align with the desire to be more present and balanced at home.

Vision: "I want to feel more connected to the people in my life."

Goal: "I will schedule one meaningful conversation or outing with a friend or family member each week, focusing on quality time without distractions."

This specific goal helps you prioritize relationships and ensures consistent action toward building deeper connections.

Vision: "I want to advance in my career and feel confident in my abilities."

Goal: "I will complete one professional development course this quarter and apply at least two new skills I learn to my current projects."

This transforms a broad career aspiration into an actionable plan that builds competence and momentum.

Vision: "I want to create a more peaceful and organized home environment."

Goal: "I will declutter one room in my house each weekend, starting with my bedroom, and donate items I no longer need."

This goal provides a clear, step-by-step approach to creating a more intentional and serene living space.

These examples emphasize how breaking down a broad vision into specific, actionable goals creates clarity and motivation for meaningful progress. It also illustrates how a single vision can have multiple goals.

3. **Break Down Big Goals:** Large goals can feel overwhelming, but breaking them down into smaller, manageable steps makes them more achievable. Reverse-engineering your goals is a powerful technique to make a big vision feel attainable. Start with the end result in mind—whether it's a personal milestone, a professional

achievement, or a creative pursuit—and then work backward to identify the smaller actions needed to bring that goal to life.

When I committed to writing this book, I knew it would be a monumental task, but I was determined to align it with the vision I had for the woman I wanted to become. As I shared earlier, signing the publishing contract was both thrilling and daunting. It symbolized more than just an agreement to write a book; it was a commitment to live in alignment with my goals, my values, and my vision. The task felt overwhelming at first—so many chapters to write, ideas to refine, and deadlines to meet. But by breaking it down into smaller, actionable steps, I transformed what felt impossible into something I could confidently tackle one day at a time.

Once I had outlined the purpose of the book and the key themes I wanted to explore, I shifted my focus to specific, smaller goals. For example, instead of thinking about "writing a book," I concentrated on writing a single chapter at a time. To make this even more manageable, I broke each chapter into sections, each with its own focus and message. By narrowing my attention to smaller pieces of the whole, I was able to maintain momentum and build confidence as I moved forward.

Another key to breaking down big goals is creating a timeline that works for you. When I looked at my overall deadline, I divided the time into phases: outlining, drafting, revising, and finalizing. Then, I set specific deadlines for each phase. For instance, I committed to completing the first draft of two chapters each month, which allowed me to focus on steady progress without becoming overwhelmed by the enormity of the final manuscript.

Each step reinforced my belief that I could achieve my goal. Finishing the outline was a milestone. Completing a chapter was another. And every time I hit a deadline, it served as proof that I was capable of turning my vision into reality. Along the way, I reminded myself that perfection wasn't the goal—progress was. Some days the words flowed effortlessly, while other days were a grind, but I kept showing up because each small action moved me closer to the bigger picture.

This approach can apply to any goal, no matter the size or scope. For instance, if your vision is to transition into a new career, breaking it down might involve researching industries, building your network, and updating your resume. Each step is manageable on its own, and together, they create a pathway to your ultimate goal.

The beauty of reverse-engineering your goals is that it shifts your focus from the overwhelming big picture to the immediate steps you can take today. Reflecting on my experience writing this book, I see how essential it was to map out each stage and create momentum through small, achievable goals. By reminding yourself of the purpose behind your goal and tying every step back to your larger vision, you stay motivated and aligned. It's not just about reaching the finish line—it's about building confidence in your ability to navigate the journey, one step at a time. Whether you're writing a book, starting a new career, or embarking on a personal transformation, breaking down your goals into actionable steps gives you the clarity and direction you need to move forward with purpose and resolve.

4. **Stay Flexible:** Flexibility isn't about giving up on your goals—it's about staying aligned with your vision, even when life throws unexpected challenges your way. When I started writing this book, I had a detailed plan and timeline, but as life often does, it didn't go exactly as expected. Between balancing my career, family, and personal responsibilities, there were moments when the timeline I envisioned needed to shift. I learned that flexibility didn't mean

abandoning my goal; it meant adapting my approach while keeping my vision in focus.

For example, there were weeks when dedicating hours to writing simply wasn't feasible. Instead of pushing myself to the brink, I broke the work into smaller, manageable pieces. Some days, that meant writing just a paragraph or jotting down ideas for future sections. By adjusting my expectations, I stayed connected to the larger purpose of the book without overwhelming myself.

Flexibility also meant reevaluating what aligned with my vision. If a chapter's tone didn't feel authentic or if a story I included no longer resonated, I allowed myself the space to pivot. These adjustments weren't setbacks; they were refinements that made the final product stronger and truer to my purpose.

Staying flexible doesn't mean you're veering off course—it means you're honoring the ebbs and flows of life while continuing to move forward. When you allow yourself the grace to adapt, you create a path that's not only sustainable but also deeply aligned with your evolving self.

Building Momentum Through Small Wins

One of the most effective ways to stay motivated and committed to your goals is to celebrate the small wins along the way. Each time you achieve a milestone, no matter how minor it may seem, you're building momentum and confidence. These small victories are more than just checkpoints; they're proof that progress is happening. They remind you that every effort counts and that you're capable of reaching your larger vision, one step at a time.

When I first started setting vision-aligned goals, I had a hard time celebrating my small wins. I thought, *Isn't this just settling for less?* or,

It's not like I've reached the finish line yet, so what's there to celebrate? But over time, I realized that this mindset was holding me back. Without acknowledging the small successes, I felt like I was constantly climbing a mountain with no end in sight. It was exhausting and discouraging. That's when I decided to shift my perspective. I began celebrating even the tiniest victories, like completing a single workout session or sticking to my evening routine for a week. These moments, though seemingly insignificant, started to fuel me. They acted as reminders that I was showing up for myself, that I was capable of staying committed, and that progress—no matter how incremental—is still progress.

Now, I actively look for opportunities to celebrate, whether it's checking an item off my to-do list or reaching a small milestone in a bigger project. Each small win is like a drop in a bucket, and over time, those drops accumulate into something meaningful and substantial. By celebrating these moments, you not only keep yourself motivated but also make the journey more enjoyable and sustainable.

Staying Committed to Your Goals

Goal-setting is just the beginning. Staying committed to your goals requires discipline, patience, and resilience. There will be days when motivation wanes, when the spark that once ignited your vision feels dim, or when life's demands seem to overshadow your aspirations. On those days, it's essential to reconnect with your "why" and remind yourself why you started this journey in the first place. Your commitment to your vision is what will sustain you when motivation alone isn't enough.

One of the strategies that has been invaluable to me is setting up accountability systems to keep my goals front and center. For me, this includes building reminders into my calendar that pop up at random times throughout the year. These reminders are my checkpoints, nudging me to evaluate my progress and reconnect with my intentions. They're often simple notes, like "How's the morning routine going?" or "Have you scheduled that self-care day yet?" or "You're halfway to your savings goal. Are you on pace to hit your target? or "It is two months out from submitting your manuscript to the editing team. Have you completed the last few chapters?" Sometimes, they serve as a gentle pat on the back when I've made progress; other times, they are the wake-up calls I need when I've veered off track.

I remember one particular reminder I had set for mid-September, a time when my schedule tends to get chaotic with work deadlines and family obligations. The alert simply read, "Are you honoring your goals for balance and joy?" At first, I dismissed it, thinking, *Of course, I am. I've been so busy!* But as I sat with it, I realized I had been so wrapped up in "busy" that I'd neglected the very things that brought me joy and balance. That little nudge from my past self was exactly what I needed to pause, recalibrate, and make adjustments. It wasn't about judgment—it was about staying connected to my vision and giving myself the opportunity to course-correct.

Sharing goals with a trusted friend or mentor has also been a powerful tool. When someone else knows your intentions, it creates an added layer of accountability. Knowing that someone else is cheering me on or asking about my progress has often motivated me to keep going, even when I've wanted to give up. Journaling has been another cornerstone of my commitment strategy. Writing down my wins, my struggles, and even my frustrations keeps me grounded in the process. It's a space to reflect, recalibrate, and remind myself of the woman I'm working to become.

As you pursue your vision-aligned goals, remember that the journey itself is where transformation happens. Growth unfolds through the striving, the learning, and even the stumbling. Embrace this process with curiosity and grace, understanding that setbacks and detours are not failures but part of your story. Each twist and turn is shaping you into the woman you want to become.

Goal-setting isn't about perfection; it's about progress. The calendar reminders, the shared goals, the journal entries—these tools are not just about tracking milestones. They're about staying present in your journey, celebrating the small wins, and finding the courage to keep going. Every step forward, no matter how small, reinforces your commitment to the life you're creating and the woman you're becoming.

Grab your journal and reflect on these questions:

- What is one vision-aligned goal, and what specific first step can you take today to move toward it? What is your why for this goal?

- What systems or tools, such as journaling or setting reminders, can you create to help hold yourself accountable to your goals?

- Reflect on a time when you stayed committed to a challenging goal. What strategies helped you push through moments of doubt or obstacles?

- When life throws unexpected challenges your way, how can you remain flexible while staying true to your vision?

Access the free workbook by scanning the QR code:

https://www.amandacahill.com/redefiningyouresources

Key Takeaways on Setting Vision-Aligned Goals

- **Align Goals with Your Vision**: Goals are most powerful when they reflect your deepest values and the future you want to create. Vision-aligned goals are stepping stones that connect your current self to the woman you aspire to become.

- **Define Your "Why"**: A clear and meaningful purpose fuels your motivation. Your "why" acts as your anchor during challenges, reminding you of the deeper significance behind your goals and driving you forward.

- **Clarity and Specificity Are Essential**: Avoid vague goals. Break down your vision into actionable, measurable, and clear steps that create momentum. For example, instead of "be healthier," set specific goals like exercising three times a week or improving sleep habits.

- **Break Big Goals into Manageable Steps**: Large goals can feel overwhelming. Reverse-engineer them into smaller, actionable milestones to make consistent progress. Celebrate each step as a victory.

- **Flexibility Is Key**: Life is unpredictable, and timelines may shift. Flexibility doesn't mean abandoning your goals; it means adjusting your approach while keeping your vision in focus.

- **Celebrate Small Wins**: Every milestone, no matter how small, builds momentum and reinforces your belief in your ability to succeed. Recognizing these wins makes the journey more enjoyable and sustainable.

- **Create Accountability Systems**: Use tools like calendar reminders, journaling, or sharing your goals with trusted friends to stay on track. These systems provide consistent motivation and help you recalibrate when needed.

- **Stay Connected to Your Vision**: Regularly reflect on your progress and your "why." This practice keeps your goals front and center, especially when motivation wanes or life feels overwhelming.

- **Progress Over Perfection**: Growth happens in the striving and the learning, not in achieving perfection. Embrace the process with curiosity and grace, knowing that every effort contributes to your transformation.

- **Transformation Happens in the Journey**: Each step, whether it's a small action or overcoming a challenge, is shaping you into the woman you are becoming. Trust the process and take pride in the progress you're making every day.

CHAPTER 9

Habits That Shape Your Identity

"We are what we repeatedly do. Excellence, then, is not an act, but a habit." – Aristotle

Habits are the building blocks of identity. They're the small, consistent actions that reinforce who you are and how you show up in the world. When you adopt habits that align with your vision and goals, you're not just creating routines—you're reshaping your identity. Every time you follow through on a habit, you're casting a vote for the person you want to become. For example, if your future self values health, every decision to move your body or nourish yourself with healthy food reinforces that identity. These choices may feel small in the moment, but over time, they shape how you see yourself and how others perceive you.

This was my reality when I began my journey to become a fit, happy, healthy mom. I knew I wanted to embody energy, vibrancy, and confidence, but the gap between where I was and where I wanted to be felt overwhelming. My energy was low, but I knew that if I focused on small, manageable actions, I could create lasting change. I began with one simple habit: walking for ten minutes each morning. At first, it felt trivial. How could ten minutes possibly make a difference? But as the weeks passed, I noticed subtle shifts. I had more energy to play with my son. My mood improved. That single habit became the foundation for more changes, like preparing healthy meals and prioritizing sleep.

Over time, these small actions compounded, transforming not only my health but also my identity. I started to see myself as a fit, happy, healthy mom—not because I had achieved perfection, but because I had consistently made choices that aligned with that vision. Each decision, no matter how small, reinforced the belief that I was capable of becoming the woman I wanted to be.

Throughout my journey, I learned that habits are far more than just routines—they're expressions of our commitment to the person we want to become. I used to think of habits as tasks to check off a list, but as I began to focus on becoming the best version of myself, I realized that habits are the building blocks of identity. Each small, intentional action contributes to the bigger picture of who you're becoming.

The Compounding Effect of Small Actions

Habits are powerful because they operate on a subconscious level. When you repeat a behavior often enough, it becomes part of your identity.

The beauty of small, disciplined actions is their compounding power over time. Each action you take builds on the last, creating a ripple effect that accelerates your progress. When you stay committed to your vision, even the smallest steps begin to add up, bringing you closer to the woman you want to become. These small actions may seem minor, but over time, they accumulate and shape how you see yourself. By choosing habits that align with your vision, you're consistently reinforcing the identity of your future self, one small step at a time. But what does this really mean? Let's dive deeper into the concept, unpack how it works, and explore how you can harness this effect in your own life.

The Power of Tiny Gains

Imagine saving money and watching it grow over time with interest. At first, the gains seem minimal—just a few extra cents or dollars—but as the interest compounds, your savings start to snowball. This is the same principle that governs small actions in your daily life. Each time you make a decision that aligns with your vision, you're making a tiny deposit into the bank of your future self. Over time, these deposits accumulate and yield incredible results.

Here's an analogy from nature: think of water dripping onto a rock. A single drop doesn't seem like much, but over time, those drops can carve through stone. It's not the strength of a single drop but the consistency of many that creates transformation. The same goes for your habits. A ten-minute walk may feel insignificant today, but if repeated daily, it can lead to improved energy, better health, and increased confidence. These changes, though gradual, become undeniable over time.

Examples of the Compounding Effect

The compounding effect is a powerful principle that touches every part of life, amplifying small, consistent actions into meaningful transformations over time. At first, these efforts may seem too small to matter, but their true power lies in their ability to accumulate and create exponential growth. Let's break this down with examples that show how this concept applies across various aspects of life:

- **Professional Growth:** Imagine you want to improve your public speaking skills. Spending just ten minutes each day practicing might feel insignificant in the beginning. Perhaps you record yourself rehearsing, study a TED Talk, or read a chapter from a book on communication. Day by day, these small investments seem inconsequential, but by the end of the year, you've dedicated over 60 hours to honing your craft. Now, you're not only more confident but also prepared to speak up in meetings or take on leadership roles that once felt out of reach. The compounding effect doesn't just improve your skills—it reshapes how you see yourself.

- **Relationships:** Relationships thrive on small, meaningful actions. Sending a thoughtful message to a friend or scheduling a quick check-in call may not seem life-changing in the moment. However, over weeks and months, these gestures build trust, deepen connections, and foster a sense of belonging. By the end of a year, you've cultivated a strong support system simply by being present and intentional in small ways.

- **Mental Health:** A five-minute gratitude practice might sound trivial compared to the challenges of daily life. But over time, this simple act rewires your brain to focus on positivity and abundance rather than stress or negativity. The shift is subtle at first—an improved mood here, a moment of clarity there. Eventually, it transforms your mindset, enhancing resilience and emotional well-being. Gratitude, when compounded daily, becomes a cornerstone of your mental health.

These examples illustrate that the compounding effect is more than just a productivity hack—it's a mindset shift. When you commit to small, consistent actions, they not only drive measurable results but also redefine who you are. Over time, you're not just achieving goals—you're becoming the person who naturally embodies those qualities.

The Psychology Behind the Compounding Effect

The compounding effect isn't just about the math of small actions adding up—it's rooted deeply in psychology, relying on two powerful principles: consistency and momentum. These principles work together to reinforce your belief in your ability to change and drive the progress that fuels transformation.

1. Consistency Creates Identity

Consistency is the quiet architect of identity. Each time you take an action, no matter how small, you're casting a vote for the person you want to become. If you consistently choose to eat healthy meals, for example, you're not just improving your diet—you're building the identity of someone who prioritizes their health. Over time, this identity shift changes how you see yourself. You're no longer someone trying to be healthy; you *are* a healthy person.

This psychological shift is incredibly motivating. When you start to see yourself as aligned with your actions, sticking to them becomes easier. Imagine the difference between saying, "I'm trying to be a fit, happy, healthy mom," and confidently declaring, "I am a fit, happy, healthy mom." That belief reinforces your commitment, making it natural to continue making choices that align with your new identity.

2. Momentum Drives Change

Momentum is the spark that turns small actions into big results. When you take even the smallest step toward your goal, it creates a sense of progress. That progress feels good, and it motivates you to take the next step. Momentum builds on itself, just like pushing a snowball down a hill. What starts as a small effort gathers energy and speed, growing larger and more powerful as it goes.

For example, imagine starting your day with a 10-minute walk. That single action might inspire you to choose a healthier breakfast, leading to more energy throughout the day. That energy fuels productivity, which makes you feel accomplished. By the end of the day, you've built a series of positive actions, all sparked by that initial, seemingly small choice.

Momentum also creates resilience. When you've built up enough forward motion, small setbacks lose their power to derail you. You've seen progress, and you know it's possible to keep going. The more you act, the more confident you become in your ability to create change—and that confidence keeps you moving forward.

The synergy between consistency and momentum is the driving force of the compounding effect. Each small action reinforces your belief in who you are becoming while creating the energy and progress needed to keep going. Together, these principles transform the seemingly insignificant into the extraordinary, proving that the psychology behind the compounding effect is just as impactful as the results it creates.

Making the Compounding Effect Work for You

The compounding effect doesn't happen by accident—it thrives on intentionality and deliberate action. By focusing on small, consistent steps, you can create meaningful change over time. Here's a simple framework to help you harness the power of the compounding effect and make it work for you:

1. **Start Small, Stay Consistent**

   The foundation of the compounding effect lies in choosing small, manageable actions that you can sustain. These actions don't need to be grand or life-changing from the start; they just need to be consistent. The key is to start where you are, with what feels doable.

   For example:

   - If your vision is to prioritize self-care, begin with something as simple as drinking a glass of water as soon as you wake up. That single action reinforces your identity as someone who values their health.

   - If your goal is to advance in your career, commit to reading one professional development article each day. That small step builds knowledge and positions you for growth.

   Starting small isn't about thinking small—it's about creating a foundation that allows you to grow without feeling overwhelmed. The smaller and more specific the habit, the easier it is to integrate into your daily life. Consistency is what transforms these small actions into powerful change.

2. **Track Your Progress**

   Consistency is easier to maintain when you can see tangible evidence of your efforts. Tracking your progress creates accountability and serves as a visual reminder of how far you've come. It doesn't have to be complicated; find a system that works for you—a journal, app, or even a simple checklist.

   For example:

   - Check off each day you exercise or meditate. Seeing a streak of checkmarks builds momentum and keeps you motivated.

   - Record the times you followed through on a new habit, like prepping healthy meals or dedicating time to a personal project.

   Tracking also turns abstract progress into something concrete. When you're feeling discouraged or wondering if your efforts are making a difference, looking back at your progress can reignite your motivation. You'll see how every small action contributes to your bigger goals.

3. **Celebrate Milestones**

   Celebrating your progress, no matter how small, reinforces your commitment and builds positive momentum. Each milestone, whether it's a week of consistent action or hitting a specific target, is a win worth acknowledging.

   For instance:

   - Reward yourself with a relaxing evening after completing a week of healthy meals or consistent workouts.

   - Share your achievements with a friend or mentor to amplify your sense of accomplishment.

Celebration isn't just about the reward; it's about pausing to recognize that you're making progress. These moments of acknowledgment remind you that every step matters and keep you energized for the journey ahead.

4. Expand Gradually

Once your initial habits feel natural and automatic, it's time to layer in new ones. Gradual expansion prevents overwhelm while building momentum. The more habits you integrate over time, the stronger your foundation becomes.

For example:

- After mastering a daily walk, add a journaling habit to reflect on your thoughts and progress.

- Once you've established a consistent morning routine, integrate a habit of reading or listening to personal development podcasts.

This approach allows you to grow at a sustainable pace. Instead of trying to overhaul your entire life at once, you're creating lasting change by focusing on one habit at a time.

5. Trust the Process

The compounding effect isn't about instant gratification—it's about long-term growth. Resist the urge to constantly check for results or expect immediate transformation. Instead, focus on showing up every day and putting in the work, knowing that the impact of your efforts will multiply over time.

Think of planting a seed. You won't see a sprout overnight, but with consistent care—water, sunlight, and patience—that seed will grow into a thriving plant. Your habits are no different. The results might not be visible right away, but they're building beneath the surface, waiting to blossom.

The beauty of the compounding effect is that it allows you to create extraordinary change through ordinary actions. By starting small, staying consistent, and trusting the process, you're paving the way for transformation that feels sustainable and deeply aligned with your vision. Every small step you take is a vote for the person you're becoming, and over time, those small steps will lead to remarkable growth. Trust in the journey and know that the seeds you're planting today will create the life you envision tomorrow.

The compounding effect is your secret weapon for transformation. It's not about taking massive leaps or achieving instant results—it's about showing up every day and trusting that your small, consistent actions will lead to big change. With every choice you make, you're casting a vote for your future self. And over time, those votes create a life that reflects your values, dreams, and identity.

So, take that first step. Start small, stay consistent, and trust in the power of the compounding effect. You'll be amazed at what's possible when you commit to the process. The woman you're becoming is already within you—let her shine through one small action at a time.

Choosing Habits That Reflect Your Vision

This is where the fun begins. Pearson's Law states that *where performance is measured, performance improves*, and it's incredibly relevant when you're working to reshape your life, one habit at a time. The idea is simple: If you want to improve, you need to keep track of your progress. By consistently measuring your habits, you bring awareness to what's working and what isn't—and with that awareness, you gain the power to pivot and make the necessary adjustments to reach your goals. So, if you're ready to take control, track your habits, and unlock the next level of your transformation, let's dive into actionable steps that will guide you on this journey.

To build habits that align with your vision, start by identifying the qualities of your future self. What does she prioritize? How does she spend her time? What values guide her choices? What goals does she have? Once you're clear on these aspects, choose habits that support and reflect this identity and the goals that go with it. Remember, habits don't have to be monumental; they just need to be consistent.

1. **Take inventory of your current habits:** Before you can create meaningful change, you need to understand where you're starting from. This begins with taking an honest inventory of your current habits—the automatic actions and routines that shape your daily life. Think of this step as shining a light on the unconscious choices you make every day. Are these habits moving you closer to your goals, or are they quietly steering you away from them?

   For example, maybe your day starts with reaching for your phone the moment you wake up, scrolling through emails or social media before you even get out of bed. On the surface, it might seem harmless, but ask yourself: *Does this habit set the tone for a productive, intentional day?* Or does it leave you feeling rushed, distracted, or reactive? Now consider how you spend your evenings. Do you find yourself zoning out in front of the TV when you could spend a few minutes journaling or planning your next day?

   These seemingly small actions are the building blocks of your life. They create patterns that either align with your goals or work against them. Taking inventory isn't about blaming yourself or feeling guilty—it's about cultivating awareness. When you know better, you can do better.

Why It's Important: You can't change what you don't acknowledge. Without recognizing your current habits, it's impossible to make intentional improvements. Awareness allows you to identify the habits that serve you and the ones that don't, empowering you to consciously shape your reality.

Actionable Step: For the next three days, keep a detailed log of your actions, from how you start your morning to how you wind down at night. Write down everything—what time you wake up, how you spend your breaks, what you do in your downtime. At the end of the third day, review your notes and ask yourself:

Which habits align with the life I want to create?

Which habits are holding me back?

This exercise isn't about judgment; it's about clarity. By understanding where you're starting from, you can begin to design habits that reflect the person you're becoming.

2. **Identify Core Habits and Goals:** Once you've taken inventory of your current habits, it's time to focus on where you want to go. This step is all about clarity: defining your dreams and breaking them down into actionable, measurable steps. It's one thing to say, "I want to be healthier" or "I want to advance in my career," but without specifics, those goals can feel overwhelming and unattainable. The secret to turning big dreams into reality lies in identifying core habits that align with your vision.

For example, if your goal is to prioritize health, a core habit might be committing to 30 minutes of movement three times a week. If your dream is to grow in your career, a habit like reading one professional development book each month or setting aside 15 minutes a day to learn a new skill can propel you forward. These core habits are the anchors of your transformation, guiding your daily actions and reinforcing the identity you're stepping into.

Why It's Important: Vague goals lead to vague results. Measurable goals, on the other hand, give you a clear direction and a way to track your progress. When you can see exactly what needs to be done and when, it reduces overwhelm and builds momentum. Each small, measurable step creates a sense of accomplishment, reinforcing your commitment and confidence as you move closer to becoming the woman you want to be.

Actionable Step: Take a few minutes to reflect on the goals that matter most to you. Then, write down three specific and measurable habits. For each one, identify the action steps needed to achieve it. For example:

- **Goal:** "I want to prioritize my health."

  o **Actions:** "I will exercise for 30 minutes, 3 times a week."

  o **Deadline:** "I will complete this for four weeks and reassess my progress."

- **Goal:** "I want to expand my professional skills."

  o **Actions:** "I will read one professional development book per month and schedule 15 minutes daily to learn a new skill."

  o **Deadline:** "By the end of three months, I will have implemented what I've learned in my current role."

Once you've identified these core habits and goals, make them part of your daily life. Track your progress, celebrate your wins, and adjust your approach as needed. These small, consistent actions are the foundation of your transformation, turning your dreams into tangible, actionable steps forward.

3. **Start Small:** Don't overwhelm yourself by trying to adopt too many new habits at once. Instead, start with one or two small, manageable actions that you can commit to daily. As these habits become ingrained, you can gradually add more.

   Why It's Important: You cannot expect to overhaul your entire life in a day. But you can slowly begin to make progress over time, with consistent effort and focus. Starting with one or two things at a time will help to build momentum.

   Actionable Step: Pick one or two habits you can focus on right *now*. What is the low-hanging fruit? Start there.

4. **Focus On and Track Your Habits with Consistency:** When it comes to building lasting habits, consistency is the secret ingredient. The power of habits doesn't come from grand gestures or intense efforts but from the steady, small actions you repeat day after day. It's not about working out for an hour once a week—it's about showing up for ten minutes every day. These small, manageable steps not only make habits sustainable but also reinforce the identity of the person you're becoming.

   Consider this: The fit, happy, healthy mom doesn't just exist because she wakes up one day and decides to overhaul her entire life. She exists because of the consistent decisions she makes every day. She chooses to drink water instead of soda. She sets aside 20 minutes to walk, even when the day feels overwhelming. Over time, these choices stack up, creating a version of her that aligns with her vision.

   This is where Pearson's Law becomes your best ally: "What is measured, improves." Tracking your habits gives you clarity and a sense of progress. It turns abstract goals into tangible, measurable steps forward. Whether you use a journal, a digital app, or even a simple checklist, tracking acts as your accountability partner, keeping you grounded and focused on your journey.

Imagine this: every evening, you check off the day's completed habits in your tracker. Maybe it's a box for drinking 8 glasses of water, a line for taking a 15-minute walk, or a star next to the pages you read from a personal development book. Seeing these small wins accumulate day after day is incredibly motivating. You're not just going through the motions—you're building momentum.

This consistency doesn't just keep you on track; it also shifts how you see yourself. Each small action is a vote for your future self. When you consistently show up for the habits you've committed to, you reinforce the belief that you are the kind of person who follows through. That belief becomes a foundation for building the life you envision.

But tracking does more than reinforce good habits—it also helps you identify areas where you might need to adjust. Maybe you notice that you're hitting your exercise goal consistently but falling short on your water intake. Or perhaps you realize that your journaling habit is thriving during the week but slipping on weekends. This awareness allows you to course-correct and refine your approach, ensuring that your efforts align with your long-term vision.

Why It's Important: Tracking isn't just about staying organized; it's about self-awareness and accountability. When you measure your progress, you're forced to confront the truth about how you're showing up for yourself. Some days, you'll see the evidence of your commitment, and it will feel amazing. Other days, you might notice a gap between your intentions and your actions—and that's okay. Tracking allows you to pivot and make adjustments, preventing small missteps from derailing your progress entirely.

Think of tracking as a roadmap for your transformation. Each entry is a breadcrumb, guiding you back to your goals and keeping your vision in focus. It's a visual reminder that you're making progress, even on days when it feels slow or insignificant.

One of the most significant benefits of tracking is the momentum it creates. Like a snowball rolling down a hill, each small win builds on the one before it, creating a ripple effect that drives you forward. This momentum isn't just motivational—it's transformative. It helps you push through tough days, reminding you that even the smallest steps matter in the grand scheme of your journey.

Actionable Step: To get started, choose a tracking method that works for your lifestyle. If you love technology, try a habit-tracking app with reminders and analytics. If you prefer analog tools, grab a notebook or print out a habit tracker. The method doesn't matter as much as the commitment to using it.

For the next two weeks, track your habits daily. Start with 1 or 2 key habits—perhaps drinking water first thing in the morning or dedicating 15 minutes to journaling—and log your progress each day. At the end of the two weeks, reflect on what worked, what didn't, and how tracking influenced your motivation.

Don't underestimate the power of these small steps. Each time you log a completed action, you're reinforcing the identity of your future self. You're proving to yourself that you're capable of growth, one small action at a time.

The Bigger Picture: Tracking your habits is about more than just reaching goals—it's about stepping into the identity of the woman you're becoming. Each time you log a completed action, you're sending yourself a powerful message: "I am committed to my growth." This simple practice isn't just a tool for productivity; it's a declaration of who you are and who you're striving to be. With every checkmark, you're proving to yourself that transformation is possible, one small step at a time.

The process of tracking is a reminder that change doesn't happen overnight. It's a gradual accumulation of small, intentional actions that, over time, lead to big results. By focusing on the process rather than the outcome, you're building a foundation of resilience and self-trust.

A Personal Reminder

When I first started using habit tracking, I didn't fully grasp its power. I thought of it as a simple way to stay organized, not realizing how much it would shape my mindset. But as I began checking off small actions—like drinking enough water, taking daily walks, or carving out time for personal growth—I noticed a shift. I felt more in control, more capable, and more aligned with the woman I wanted to become.

Each mark on my tracker was more than just a task completed—it was a promise kept to myself. And with each promise, my confidence grew. Tracking became a ritual of self-accountability, a way to celebrate my progress and stay connected to my vision.

Remember, the goal isn't perfection—it's progress. There will be days when you miss a habit or feel unmotivated. That's okay. What matters is that you keep showing up, logging your efforts, and trusting the process. Over time, those small actions will compound, transforming not only your habits but also your sense of self.

With each day you track, you're building a life that aligns with your vision. You're not just hoping for change—you're creating it, one habit at a time. You're sending a message to yourself that you are committed to your growth. And with that commitment, you can achieve anything.

Transforming Habits Into a Lifestyle

The ultimate goal of building habits is to weave them into the fabric of your daily life so seamlessly that they become second nature—an intrinsic part of who you are. This isn't about checking off a to-do list;

it's about creating a life that reflects your values and aspirations. When habits transform into lifestyle choices, they cease to feel like obligations and start to feel like natural extensions of your identity.

Think of it like learning to ride a bike. At first, every movement requires effort and concentration. You're hyper aware of balancing, pedaling, and steering all at once. But as you practice, those actions become automatic. Eventually, you're riding without a second thought, fully immersed in the joy of the experience. The same is true for habits. Initially, they may feel forced or awkward, but over time, they integrate into your life effortlessly.

The beauty of habits is that they don't stay static. They evolve and expand as you grow. Once my initial habits became automatic, I layered on new ones. I added more mindful eating, short bursts of strength training, and moments of gratitude reflection into my day. These additions didn't feel overwhelming because the foundation was already in place.

Embracing the Journey of Habit Building

Building habits isn't a straight path, and it's certainly not a race. There will be days when you feel energized and motivated, and days when sticking to your habits feels like climbing a mountain. It's in those challenging moments that the true power of consistency shines. Missing a day doesn't mean failure—it's just a reminder to realign and keep moving forward.

Transformation requires patience and grace. It's easy to fall into the trap of expecting immediate results, but real growth happens in the process. Every small action, every choice to show up, is an investment in the woman you are becoming. Even on the days when progress feels invisible, trust that those small steps are building something extraordinary.

This journey isn't about perfection; it's about persistence. Embrace the messiness of it, the trial and error, and the moments of self-discovery. Celebrate every win, no matter how small, because each one brings you closer to your vision. Habits aren't just about what you do—they're about who you're becoming.

As you continue to build habits that align with your future self, know that you're not just creating routines. You're creating a lifestyle that reflects the best version of you—a lifestyle that feels authentic, empowering, and deeply fulfilling. Honor your progress, trust in the process, and celebrate the incredible woman you're becoming, one intentional habit at a time.

Grab your journal and reflect on these questions:

- What habits align with the life you want to create?

- Which habits are holding you back?

- What are one or two habits you can focus on right *now* to bring you closer to the woman you want to become?

- What are you going to use to track your habits?

Access the free workbook by scanning the QR code:

https://www.amandacahill.com/redefiningyouresources

Key Takeaways on Habits That Shape Your Identity

- **Habits Define Identity**: Habits are the building blocks of who you are. Every small, consistent action you take is a vote for the person you want to become. They're not just routines; they reflect your commitment to your vision and values.

- **Start Small and Build Consistency**: Begin with manageable actions that align with your future self. Small, consistent efforts create momentum and build confidence, allowing habits to evolve naturally into a lifestyle.

- **The Power of the Compounding Effect**: Tiny, disciplined actions add up over time, creating exponential growth. Whether it's a daily walk, a gratitude practice, or professional development, these small efforts compound into meaningful transformations.

- **Track Your Progress**: Use tools like journals, habit trackers, or apps to measure your efforts. Tracking not only builds self-awareness but also keeps you accountable and motivated, reinforcing your belief in the transformation process.

- **Celebrate Small Wins**: Recognizing and celebrating even minor milestones builds momentum and keeps you motivated. These small celebrations reinforce your commitment and make the process more enjoyable.

- **Focus on Progress, Not Perfection**: Transformation happens in the process. Embrace the journey, including setbacks, and keep showing up. Progress over time will lead to lasting change.

- **Expand Gradually**: Once your initial habits are established, add new ones that align with your evolving goals. This layering approach builds a strong foundation for long-term transformation.

- **Trust the Process**: Habits take time to build, and their effects often start small. Trust that consistent effort will yield results, even when progress feels invisible.

- **Habits as a Lifestyle**: Over time, habits should feel like a natural part of who you are. They transform from tasks to an integral part of your identity and lifestyle, reflecting the person you're becoming.

CHAPTER 10

Commitments Over Feelings

*"Your feelings don't always tell you the truth. But
your commitments do. Stay the course."*
– Christine Caine

One of the greatest challenges in any transformational journey is learning to honor your commitments more than your emotions. On the surface, this might seem straightforward but think about how often you've let fleeting feelings dictate your actions. You might promise yourself you'll go for a run, finish that passion project, or dedicate time to self-care, but when the moment arrives, you feel tired, stressed, or simply not in the mood. It's easy to rationalize: *I'll do it tomorrow,* or, *I deserve a break today.*

But here's the truth: Transformation doesn't wait for convenience. It doesn't thrive on the whims of your emotions. The life you want and the woman you aspire to become aren't built on fleeting bursts of motivation but on a foundation of consistent, disciplined action. Honoring your commitments—especially when it's hard—is where real growth happens.

This is a lesson I had to learn firsthand. Early in my journey to becoming a fit, happy, healthy mom, I found myself frequently negotiating with my goals. I'd tell myself, *It's been a long day; I'll exercise tomorrow.* Or, *This one unhealthy snack won't make a difference.* While each choice seemed small, over time, they added up to a pattern of inconsistency that kept me stuck. It wasn't until I committed to honoring my promises, no matter how I felt in the moment, that I started to see real progress.

If you wait for motivation to strike, you'll always find reasons to delay. Motivation is fleeting; it's unreliable. Discipline, on the other hand, is a skill you can cultivate. It's what allows you to show up even when you don't feel like it. And showing up—day after day—is what leads to lasting transformation.

When faced with a choice, I started asking myself a simple but powerful question: *What would my future self do in this situation?* Would she hit snooze and skip the workout, or would she push through, knowing the long-term benefits? Would she avoid a challenging task, or would she tackle it head-on because she's committed to her growth? The answer was always clear when I focused on the woman I wanted to become, not the woman I was in that fleeting moment of discomfort. This practice of envisioning my future self became a game-changer. It shifted my perspective and gave me clarity in moments of doubt. It wasn't just about immediate action—it was about aligning every decision with the vision of who I wanted to be. Each time I chose discipline over convenience, I reinforced my belief in my ability to change and strengthen the foundation for my transformation.

It's important to acknowledge that this isn't about ignoring your emotions. Your feelings are valid and worth exploring, but they don't have to dictate your actions. Instead, let your commitments guide you. By choosing to act in alignment with your values and goals, you're training yourself to prioritize what matters most, even when it's uncomfortable.

Honoring your commitments over your emotions isn't easy, but it's one of the most powerful tools you have for transformation. Each time you follow through—each time you choose to push past resistance—you're proving to yourself that you're capable, resilient, and worthy of the life you envision. Remember: The woman you want to become is watching. What choice will you make for her today?

Why Feelings Can Be Misleading

Our feelings often feel urgent and persuasive, convincing us to make decisions based on the emotion of the moment. But as powerful as they are, feelings can also be misleading. They can tether us to the status quo, even when that status quo is uncomfortable or no longer serves us. And they can trick us into acting in ways that are out of alignment with who we truly want to be. I learned this lesson the hard way when I faced one of the toughest professional setbacks of my life: a bad performance review.

As I mentioned in an earlier chapter, receiving that bad performance review at work was devastating. I'd always prided myself on my work ethic and the quality of what I delivered, so to hear that I wasn't meeting expectations shook me to my core. My initial reaction was anger and defensiveness. I felt wronged and misunderstood. My mind spiraled with thoughts like, *They don't appreciate me,* and *This is unfair.* Those feelings were heavy, and they lingered, affecting how I showed up at work each day. I started to withdraw in meetings, avoid taking initiative, and put in just enough effort to get by. My emotions convinced me to retreat and protect myself, but in doing so, I became someone I didn't want to be—someone disengaged, resentful, and stagnant.

Looking back, I realize how misleading those feelings were. They were keeping me stuck, holding me back from stepping into the potential I knew I had. My anger and defensiveness might have felt justified at the time, but they weren't helping me grow or improve. In fact, they were doing the opposite: They were reinforcing the very narrative that I wasn't capable of more. Those feelings were pulling me deeper into the status quo, a place I knew I didn't want to stay.

The turning point came when I began to question whether my feelings were truly serving me. I asked myself, *Are these emotions helping me become the person I want to be, or are they keeping me small?* The answer was clear. My feelings were trapping me in a cycle of self-pity and inaction, and I knew I had to break free.

That's when I decided to show up differently. Instead of letting my emotions dictate my actions, I chose to honor my commitment to becoming a better professional. I started asking myself, *What would the version of me who excels at work do in this situation?* She wouldn't sulk or withdraw. She would take the feedback as an opportunity to grow. She would push herself to be more present, more proactive, and more engaged.

Showing up differently wasn't easy. Every day, I had to fight the urge to retreat into old patterns of thinking. I had to remind myself that feelings, while valid, weren't always reliable indicators of what I should do next. Some days, I still felt frustrated or unmotivated, but I made the conscious choice to act in alignment with my values and my vision instead of my emotions. I started contributing more in meetings, reaching out to colleagues for collaboration, and seeking ways to improve my performance. Slowly but surely, I began to rebuild my confidence—and my reputation.

This experience taught me a powerful lesson: Feelings are often temporary, but the actions we take in response to them can have lasting impacts. If I had continued to let my emotions dictate my behavior, I would have remained stuck in a place of unhappiness and frustration. But by choosing to act in alignment with my goals, I was able to break free from that cycle and move forward.

Feelings can play tricks on your mind, convincing you that staying comfortable is the best option. But growth rarely happens in the comfort zone. When faced with emotions that make you want to stay where you are, pause and ask yourself, *Is this feeling serving me? Is it helping me move closer to my goals, or is it holding me back?*

By making the choice to honor your commitments over your feelings, you're taking control of your journey. You're choosing progress over stagnation, growth over status quo. It's not always easy, but it's always worth it. And the more you practice, the more you'll realize that your commitments are far more powerful than any temporary emotion.

The Importance of Self-Trust

Self-trust is the foundation upon which confidence, resilience, and growth are built. When you honor your commitments—no matter how small—you're sending yourself a powerful message: *I can trust myself to show up.* Each time you follow through on a promise, you reinforce the belief that you are reliable, capable, and in control of your journey. This self-trust becomes a wellspring of motivation, especially during moments when the road ahead feels uncertain or challenging.

Imagine telling a friend you'll meet them for coffee at 9 a.m. and then canceling at the last minute without explanation. Over time, they'd stop believing in your word. The same thing happens internally when you constantly break promises to yourself. Each time you tell yourself you'll start that workout plan, finish that project, or stick to a new habit—and then don't—you chip away at the trust you have in your own reliability. It creates a narrative that you can't depend on yourself, which, over time, fosters frustration, self-doubt, and a sense of helplessness.

I've experienced this firsthand. There were times in my life when I made countless promises to myself—*I'll eat healthier this week,* or *I'll finally call that client today*—only to let feelings of procrastination or doubt derail my plans. Each broken promise left me feeling less confident in my ability to create real change. I'd think, *Why even bother? I always end up back where I started.* It wasn't until I consciously began to prioritize honoring my commitments, no matter how I felt in the moment, that I began to rebuild my sense of self-trust. The shift began with small, manageable commitments. I promised myself I'd drink a glass of water every morning before coffee. Simple, right? But that small action was significant—it was a promise I could keep. And each time I followed through, it was like casting a vote for the woman I wanted to become. The more I kept these small promises, the more I believed in my ability to tackle bigger ones. It wasn't just about drinking water—it was about proving to myself that I could depend on myself.

On the flip side, when you let feelings dictate your actions, you reinforce the idea that you can't trust yourself. Skipping a workout because you're tired, postponing a task because you're overwhelmed, or abandoning a goal because it feels inconvenient sends the message that your commitments are negotiable. Over time, this erodes your sense of self-respect, leaving you questioning your ability to follow through on anything.

Rebuilding self-trust doesn't require grand gestures or drastic overhauls. It starts with small, intentional actions. Begin by making promises you know you can keep. Maybe it's setting aside ten minutes each evening to reflect on your day or committing to taking the stairs instead of the elevator once a day. These small wins create momentum, reminding you that you are someone who honors your word.

As your self-trust grows, so does your confidence. You begin to approach challenges with a mindset of "I can do this" instead of "What if I fail?" Trusting yourself isn't about perfection—it's about consistency. It's about showing up for yourself, even on the tough days, and proving that you're capable of prioritizing your growth and goals.

When you nurture self-trust, you're also building self-respect. You're acknowledging that your promises to yourself matter just as much—if not more—than the promises you make to others. This shift empowers you to stay committed to your vision, no matter what emotions arise along the way. And as you continue to honor your commitments, you'll find that self-trust becomes not just a motivator, but a cornerstone of the woman you're becoming.

Strategies for Honoring Your Commitments

1. Define Your Non-Negotiables

Non-negotiables are the habits or actions you commit to honoring, no matter how you feel in the moment. These are your guiding principles—the actions that keep you aligned with your vision, even when resistance or doubt creeps in. Clearly defining your non-negotiables gives you a framework for staying committed and provides stability in moments of uncertainty.

When I received the poor performance review at work, I could have let the emotions take over. It would have been easy to disengage, do the bare minimum, and blame external circumstances. But I knew that wouldn't help me grow. I had to decide what my non-negotiables would be moving forward.

One of those non-negotiables became showing up each day with intentionality and a commitment to improvement. That meant actively contributing to meetings, delivering work I could be proud of, and seeking feedback to ensure I was on the right track. These weren't grand gestures—they were small, consistent actions that demonstrated my dedication. No matter how uncomfortable it felt, I refused to let my emotions dictate my performance. Over time, those non-negotiables became the foundation for rebuilding trust and confidence in myself.

Your non-negotiables might look different—maybe it's dedicating time to your personal growth or committing to a daily self-care practice. Whatever they are, make them clear and unwavering. When you define your non-negotiables, you give yourself a roadmap for honoring your commitments, regardless of the circumstances.

2. Plan for Resistance

Resistance isn't a matter of *if*—it's a matter of *when*. Life is full of distractions, unexpected challenges, and moments when your energy or confidence falters. The key to honoring your commitments lies in anticipating these obstacles and creating a plan to overcome them.

With the poor performance review, the resistance I felt wasn't physical—it was emotional. I doubted myself, felt embarrassed, and struggled with the fear of judgment from my colleagues and supervisors. The thought of going back to work each day felt daunting. My emotions whispered that staying small, blending into the background, or avoiding challenges altogether was the safer route. But deep down, I knew that wouldn't serve me in the long run.

To counteract that resistance, I had to plan my approach intentionally. I reminded myself of the commitment I had made to my professional growth. Instead of retreating, I focused on tangible actions that would rebuild my confidence. I reviewed the feedback objectively and identified specific areas for improvement. I prepared for meetings thoroughly, practiced delivering updates with clarity, and made a point to contribute to team discussions—even when it felt uncomfortable.

One of the most powerful strategies I implemented was setting a clear intention for each workday. Before walking into the office, I'd ask myself: *How can I show up as the professional I want to be today?* This simple question shifted my focus from the weight of the past to the potential of the present.

Planning for resistance isn't about eliminating obstacles entirely— it's about lessening their impact. Whether it's setting small goals to regain momentum or preparing strategies to counteract self-doubt, having a plan makes it easier to face challenges head-on. Resistance will always be there, but with a proactive mindset, you can move through it with confidence and purpose.

3. Reframe Setbacks

Setbacks are inevitable, but they don't have to derail your progress. Instead of viewing them as failures, see them as opportunities to learn, adjust, and strengthen your commitment. The way you respond to setbacks says more about your character than the setback itself.

When I received the bad performance review, it felt like a personal failure. My initial reaction was to feel defeated and question my abilities. Those emotions were powerful, and for a moment, they almost convinced me to give up trying altogether. But then I took a step back and reframed the experience. Instead of letting it define me, I asked myself: *What can I learn from this?* and *How can I use this as a stepping stone to improve?* I began to approach each piece of feedback as an opportunity for growth. If I missed a deadline or delivered something below expectations, I didn't spiral into self-criticism. Instead, I evaluated what went wrong and identified how I could prevent it in the future. Was I managing my time poorly? Was I unclear about expectations? By reframing the situation, I turned what felt like a career low point into one of the most pivotal periods of growth in my professional life.

Reframing setbacks isn't about dismissing your feelings; it's about not letting those feelings control your actions. When you shift your perspective and look for lessons, setbacks become stepping stones, not roadblocks. They build resilience, strengthen your resolve, and bring you closer to the person you're working to become.

Building Resilience Through Commitment

Resilience is the ability to keep moving forward, even when faced with challenges, setbacks, or moments of doubt. It's not something you're born with—it's something you build, step by step, decision by decision. And one of the most effective ways to build resilience is by choosing commitment over comfort. Every time you honor a commitment, even when it feels difficult or inconvenient, you're proving to yourself that you have the strength to persevere, even when the path feels uncertain.

Resilience doesn't mean you're immune to the emotions that come with challenges. Believe me, there were still days when the weight of that review hung over me. But I had already committed to showing up, and with each day that I did, I was reminded that the setback didn't define me. What mattered more was how I responded to it. Resilience isn't about never feeling doubt or fear—it's about showing up despite those feelings.

Each morning, I reminded myself of my commitment to not let this performance review dictate the rest of my career. I started small. On the hardest days, I broke my responsibilities into manageable steps, focusing on the next task in front of me rather than the overwhelming big picture. Some days, that meant completing just one task with excellence. Other days, it meant reaching out for feedback, even though it made me uncomfortable. With every action, I built momentum and regained confidence. Over time, those small wins began to add up. I noticed how showing up each day not only improved my performance but also rebuilt my self-trust. Each time I chose action over avoidance, I was proving to myself that I had the strength to navigate difficult situations. That's what resilience is: Trusting yourself to handle the hard things and moving forward, one step at a time.

And here's the incredible part: That resilience I built during one of the toughest periods of my career didn't just help me overcome the performance review—it became the foundation for my greatest professional achievement. As I continued to honor my commitment to growth, I began to see myself as someone capable of achieving more. I didn't stop at just improving my performance; I set my sights higher. I started applying for roles that aligned with the confident, capable version of myself I was becoming.

Eventually, that commitment led to a breakthrough. I landed an executive-level position at a new company, a role that challenged me to grow even further and allowed me to step fully into the professional woman I had envisioned. Looking back, I know that landing that role wasn't just about having the right qualifications or being in the right place at the right time—it was about the resilience I had cultivated. That resilience reminded me that the performance review didn't define me. It showed me that I had the power to shape my career and my future, no matter what obstacles I faced.

This journey taught me that resilience isn't just about surviving setbacks—it's about using them as stepping stones to build the life you want. When you stick to your commitments, even in the face of doubt or fear, you're creating a foundation for transformation. You're proving to yourself that no setback can hold you back from becoming the woman you're meant to be. By choosing commitment over comfort, you're not just overcoming challenges—you're paving the way for opportunities that once felt out of reach. And that is the true power of resilience.

Embracing a Lifestyle of Commitment

Honoring your commitments isn't just something you do—it's who you are. It's a lifestyle that reflects your values, dreams, and integrity. It's about showing up for yourself every single day, even when it's hard, and proving through your actions that you're worthy of the life you're working to create.

When you embrace a lifestyle of commitment, you're choosing to align your daily decisions with your vision. It means prioritizing growth over convenience, integrity over excuses, and resilience over comfort. This isn't about making grand gestures or achieving instant success; it's about the quiet, consistent choices that compound over time to create meaningful transformation. Every time you honor a commitment, no matter how small, you're reinforcing the belief that you have the power to shape your life and become the woman you've always envisioned.

For me, embracing a lifestyle of commitment meant redefining how I approached setbacks and challenges. When I faced that tough performance review at work, it would have been easy to let my feelings dictate my response. However, choosing commitment over my emotions showed me what was possible when I stayed true to my vision. The resilience I built during that period didn't just help me navigate the immediate challenge—it paved the way for greater opportunities and deeper self-trust. That's the beauty of commitment: It's not just about where you are today, but about who you're becoming tomorrow.

This lifestyle of commitment empowers you to take control of your journey, even when the road feels long or uncertain. It helps you anchor yourself in your purpose, giving you the strength to navigate setbacks and the courage to pursue your dreams. Living this way isn't about perfection—it's about persistence. It's about recognizing that every small action, every decision to honor your commitments, is moving you closer to the woman you're meant to be.

As you continue on this path, remind yourself that transformation isn't a one-time event; it's a lifelong journey. Some days will feel effortless, while others will require grit and determination. Embrace the process, celebrate the progress, and trust that each small step matters. By honoring your commitments, you're not just creating change—you're embodying the qualities of the woman you've always wanted to be.

The power to create lasting transformation lies in your ability to stay committed, to trust in the process, and to believe in your capacity for growth. As you embrace this lifestyle of commitment, know that every choice you make is a step toward the life you've envisioned. With courage, consistency, and self-belief, you can create a life that reflects your values and dreams—a life that feels purposeful, authentic, and truly yours.

Grab your journal and reflect on these questions:

- When I think about the woman I am becoming, does she let her emotions get in the way of taking action?

- What commitments have I made to myself recently, and how consistently have I honored them?

- How do my emotions currently influence my actions?

- What are my non-negotiables? How can I make those a consistent part of my routine?

- When have I allowed setbacks to derail my progress, and how can I reframe future challenges as opportunities for growth?

- What does self-trust mean to me?

Access the free workbook by scanning the QR code:

https://www.amandacahill.com/redefiningyouresources

Key Takeaways on How to Honor Your Commitments Over Your Feelings

- **Commitment Over Emotions**: Transformation requires prioritizing your commitments over fleeting feelings. Motivation may waver, but discipline and consistency will drive lasting change.

- **Feelings Can Be Misleading**: While feelings are valid, they can tether you to the status quo or lead to inaction. Instead, ask yourself if your emotions are serving your goals or holding you back, and choose actions that align with your vision.

- **The Power of Self-Trust**: Honoring your commitments builds self-trust, which is foundational for confidence and resilience. Each promise kept strengthens your belief in your ability to follow through and create meaningful change.

- **Define Non-Negotiables**: Set clear, unwavering commitments that align with your values and vision. These non-negotiables provide a roadmap for staying focused, even when challenges arise.

- **Plan for Resistance**: Anticipate obstacles and create strategies to overcome them. Resistance is inevitable, but having a proactive mindset ensures you can push through and remain committed.

- **Reframe Setbacks**: View setbacks as opportunities for growth, not failures. Reflect on what you can learn and use these lessons to strengthen your resolve and resilience.

- **Build Resilience Through Action**: Resilience grows through consistent, disciplined actions, even in the face of doubt or fear. Each decision to honor your commitments reinforces your ability to navigate challenges and create change.

- **Embrace a Lifestyle of Commitment**: Transformation is a journey, not a one-time event. Living a committed life means aligning your actions with your values daily, embracing persistence over perfection, and trusting that each small step contributes to your growth.

CHAPTER 11

The 'One Thing' Philosophy

"The difference between successful people and really successful people is that really successful people say no to almost everything." – Warren Buffett

Life often feels like a juggling act. Between personal goals, professional responsibilities, family commitments, and everything else pulling for your attention, it's easy to feel overwhelmed. You have big dreams, but they're often buried under the weight of daily demands. How do you break free from this cycle? How do you move forward when everything feels equally important?

The answer lies in a simple yet powerful idea: focusing on *One Thing*. This philosophy, outlined in the best-selling book *The One Thing* by Gary Keller and Jay Papasan, teaches that success and transformation don't come from doing more—they come from doing what matters most. By identifying the single most impactful habit or action aligned with your vision and committing to it, you create clarity, momentum, and lasting change.

This chapter isn't about adding more to your plate. It's about simplifying your approach, so you can focus on what will truly move the needle in your life. When you embrace the *One Thing* philosophy, you're giving yourself permission to let go of the noise and zero in on the actions that matter most.

I didn't fully understand the power of this philosophy until I hit a crossroads in my own life. As I've mentioned throughout this book, after having my son, I struggled to find my footing. I felt exhausted, out of shape, and like I had lost touch with the woman I wanted to be. I knew I wanted to show up as a healthier, more confident, happier version of myself—not just for myself, but for my family. But the gap between where I was and where I wanted to be felt insurmountable. Everywhere I turned, there was another demand on my time, another area of my life that needed attention. The idea of tackling it all at once was paralyzing.

That's when I realized I needed to focus on just *one thing*. The first thing I knew I could control was how I showed up for my health. If I could prioritize my well-being, I believed it would have a trickle effect into every other area of my life. But even within the realm of health, I had to simplify further. It wasn't about trying to overhaul my entire diet or commit to an intense fitness program right away. My *One Thing* became prioritizing protein at every meal. That was it. It felt manageable, and it gave me something specific to focus on without overwhelming myself.

What I didn't expect was how that one simple habit would transform not just my health, but my identity. By committing to protein at every meal, I started noticing changes in my energy and satiety. That small win made me feel capable, which motivated me to take the next step. I began to incorporate more movement into my day—starting with short walks around the neighborhood. As I built momentum, my identity began to shift. I no longer saw myself as someone who was tired and stuck. I started to see myself as someone who prioritized health, and that belief fueled my actions.

Over time, my focus on protein expanded into something much bigger. I became someone who lifts weights 4–5 times a week before work, walks over 10,000 steps a day, and genuinely enjoys moving her body. What started as a simple dietary habit laid the foundation for a lifestyle of discipline, resilience, and self-care. That discipline spilled over into other areas of my life, giving me the confidence to start a podcast and write this very book. The *One Thing* philosophy wasn't just about achieving a single goal—it was about becoming the woman I wanted to be, one small, intentional step at a time.

This is the beauty of the *One Thing* philosophy: it doesn't ask you to do everything at once. Instead, it helps you focus on the *one* habit or action that will create the greatest impact. It's not about working harder—it's about working smarter, putting your energy into the actions that will generate the most meaningful results.

Focusing on your *One Thing* simplifies decision-making, reduces overwhelm, and helps you build momentum. It teaches you to trust the process, even when progress feels slow, because you know that each small action is moving you closer to your vision. For me, starting with protein at every meal may have seemed like a small and insignificant step, but it was the first domino in a chain reaction that transformed my health, my confidence, and my life.

The same is possible for you. Whether your vision is to advance in your career, improve your relationships, or cultivate greater self-care, the key is to start small and focus on what matters most. When you identify your *One Thing* and commit to it, you're creating a foundation for growth that will ripple into every other area of your life.

The *One Thing* philosophy works because it harnesses the power of clarity and simplicity. When everything feels equally important, it's easy to freeze, unsure of where to start. But by identifying the one action that aligns most closely with your vision and values, you're cutting through the noise and giving yourself permission to focus. Transformation doesn't come from doing everything—it comes from doing the right thing.

Why the 'One Thing' Philosophy Works

The *One Thing* philosophy works because it addresses one of the most significant obstacles to progress: distraction. In today's fast-paced world, it's easy to feel pulled in a dozen directions at once. With countless priorities competing for your attention, your energy becomes scattered, leaving you feeling busy but not truly productive. The *One Thing* approach flips this narrative by encouraging you to focus all your energy on a single high-impact priority at a time.

Why does this approach work so effectively? Because success is sequential, not simultaneous. Imagine lining up a series of dominoes. When you focus on tipping over just the first one, it creates momentum, knocking over the next, then the next, until the entire row falls. This is the power of focusing on *One Thing*—it generates a ripple effect that builds momentum over time. But try to tip all the dominoes at once? That's where burnout and stagnation occur.

One of the most compelling aspects of the *One Thing* philosophy is how it creates clarity. When you know exactly what matters most, decision-making becomes easier. This clarity cuts through the overwhelm that comes from juggling too many priorities. Instead of trying to do everything, you can confidently say no to what doesn't matter and say yes to what does. This shift not only streamlines your focus but also reduces the mental load of constantly debating where to direct your energy.

Another reason the *One Thing* philosophy works is that it challenges the myth of multitasking. Research shows that multitasking isn't as efficient as it seems; in reality, switching between tasks dilutes your focus and increases mental fatigue. By concentrating on a single, high-priority action, you enter a state of flow—a place where your best work happens because all your attention is directed toward one meaningful goal.

The sequential nature of the *One Thing* philosophy also highlights the compounding effect of small, consistent actions, which we discussed earlier. Every time you act on your *One Thing*, you're not just making progress—you're building a foundation for exponential growth. Think about it: each domino you tip adds to the momentum, making it easier to tackle the next challenge. Over time, this compounding effect leads to transformative results, far greater than what could be achieved through scattered efforts.

Consider this: Focusing on your *One Thing* doesn't just make you more productive—it builds confidence. Every time you follow through on your commitment, you're proving to yourself that you're capable of creating change. This consistent alignment with your priorities reinforces self-trust and strengthens your belief in your ability to achieve your vision.

For example, let's say your *One Thing* is improving your financial well-being. By focusing on a single action, such as setting a specific monthly savings goal, you're building a habit that supports your overall financial stability. The clarity of this focus allows you to see tangible progress, which fuels your motivation. As saving a set amount each month becomes second nature, it creates a domino effect, influencing other areas of your financial life—you might become more mindful of your spending, which leads to smarter budgeting, which in turn reduces financial stress and gives you greater freedom. The compounding benefits of this single, focused action highlight why the *One Thing* works so powerfully.

The philosophy also works because it empowers you to embrace simplicity in a world that often rewards busyness. Instead of chasing multiple goals simultaneously, you're asked to focus on the one action that will make the biggest impact. This approach fosters a deeper sense of intentionality. It's not about doing more; it's about doing what matters most.

Lastly, the *One Thing* philosophy works because it aligns with how our brains are wired. The human brain thrives on focus and clarity. When we concentrate on a single priority, we activate neural pathways that strengthen our ability to concentrate and execute tasks effectively. Over time, this practice rewires our brains for success, making it easier to stay disciplined and focused.

In essence, the *One Thing* philosophy is a powerful antidote to the overwhelm of modern life. It provides a clear roadmap for moving forward, one step at a time. By focusing on what truly matters, you unlock the ability to create meaningful change without spreading yourself too thin. This singular focus not only simplifies your approach but also amplifies your results, making transformation achievable, sustainable, and deeply rewarding.

Finding Your *One Thing*

Identifying your *One Thing* is a deeply personal process, requiring intentionality and focus. This isn't about picking something arbitrarily or defaulting to what feels easiest. It's about pinpointing the habit, action, or focus that will create the greatest impact in your life—a keystone that sets everything else in motion. Here's how to uncover it:

1. **Revisit Your Vision**

    The journey to finding your *One Thing* starts with clarity about your vision. Think back to the future self you've envisioned—the woman you're becoming. Ask yourself: *What does she prioritize? What habits and actions define her life?*

    For example, if your vision involves becoming a healthier, more vibrant version of yourself, your *One Thing* might center around physical well-being, like committing to regular movement or focusing on nutrition. If your vision includes advancing in your career, your focus might shift to mastering a skill that opens doors, such as getting an advanced degree, improving your public speaking, or taking leadership development courses.

When I began my journey to becoming a fit, happy, healthy mom, my vision was crystal clear. I saw a version of myself who felt strong, had energy for my son, and radiated confidence. As I mentioned earlier, I knew health was the foundation for that vision, and so my *One Thing* became prioritizing protein at every meal. That small focus didn't just support my physical health—it created ripple effects in my energy, mindset, and self-discipline, laying the groundwork for deeper transformation.

Your vision serves as the compass pointing you toward what truly matters. Use it as your guide when choosing the *One Thing* that will align your actions with the life you're building.

2. Ask the Key Question

In *The One Thing*, Keller and Papasan pose a powerful question: "What's the one thing I can do such that by doing it, everything else will be easier or unnecessary?" This question is a game-changer. It forces you to think strategically about leverage. The right *One Thing* creates momentum, unlocking progress in multiple areas of your life.

Let's say your goal is to reduce stress. Instead of tackling everything at once—organizing your calendar, overhauling your habits, and starting a workout routine—focus on the keystone habit that could shift everything. Perhaps your *One Thing* is dedicating 10 minutes a day to mindfulness. That single practice could reduce anxiety, improve focus, and enhance your productivity, making other stress-reduction efforts easier to manage.

The beauty of this question lies in its simplicity. It narrows your focus to what truly matters, cutting through the noise of competing priorities. Write it down, reflect on it, and let it guide you to the action that will create the greatest ripple effect in your life.

3. Look for Alignment

Your *One Thing* isn't just about practicality—it's about alignment. It should resonate with your values and goals. Choosing an action that feels meaningful and connected to your vision makes it easier to stay committed, even when the journey gets tough.

Ask yourself: *Does this action feel authentic to me? Will it move me closer to the woman I want to be and the life I want to create?* If the answer is yes, you're on the right track. If it feels forced or disconnected, you might need to dig deeper.

For example, when I chose to prioritize protein, it wasn't just a practical decision—it aligned with my values of health and vitality. It wasn't about dieting or achieving an aesthetic goal; it was about nourishing my body so I could show up fully in all areas of my life. That alignment made it easier to stay consistent, even on the days when it felt inconvenient.

Remember, your *One Thing* should inspire you, not drain you. It's a priority that fuels your growth and keeps you grounded in what matters most.

4. Test and Refine

Choosing your *One Thing* isn't about getting it perfect from the start—it's about starting somewhere and being willing to adapt as you go. Once you've identified an action or habit that feels impactful, commit to it fully and track the results. Pay attention to how it influences your progress and whether it creates the momentum you hoped for.

If it's working, keep going. If it's not, don't be afraid to refine your focus. Maybe your initial *One Thing* was exercising for 30 minutes every day, but you found it hard to maintain. Instead of abandoning the goal, adjust it—perhaps committing to a 15-minute walk is more sustainable. The goal isn't perfection; it's progress.

The process of finding your *One Thing* is dynamic. As you grow and your priorities evolve, your focus may shift. That's okay. The key is to stay open, curious, and intentional about what truly moves the needle in your life.

Finding your *One Thing* isn't about doing more; it's about doing what matters most. It's about identifying the single action that aligns with your vision, resonates with your values, and creates a ripple effect that propels you forward. By taking the time to uncover your *One Thing* and committing to it fully, you're giving yourself the gift of focus, clarity, and exponential growth. Remember: The woman you're becoming is shaped by the decisions you make today. Choose your *One Thing*, and watch how it transforms not just your actions, but your entire life.

Making Your *One Thing* a Lifestyle

The real magic of the *One Thing* philosophy isn't just in identifying what matters most—it's in weaving that focus into the fabric of your daily life. It's not about adding another task to an already full schedule; it's about creating a lifestyle that prioritizes your *One Thing* above distractions, noise, and competing demands. Here's how to take that single, impactful focus and turn it into a foundation for transformation:

1. **Treat It Like a Non-Negotiable**

   Your *One Thing* isn't a casual commitment or just another item on your to-do list. It's the cornerstone of your growth and the anchor for everything else you want to achieve. To make it stick, you need to treat it as sacred—something that cannot be skipped, postponed, or deprioritized.

When I committed to my health as my *One Thing*, I had to make it non-negotiable. It wasn't about squeezing it in if I had time—it was about creating time for it, no matter what. At first, my focus was small and specific: prioritizing protein at every meal. That single action was manageable, and I could consistently show up for it. It became something I could count on myself to do, even on chaotic days.

The beauty of treating your *One Thing* as non-negotiable is that it builds self-trust. Each time you honor that commitment, you reinforce the belief that you're capable of following through. Whether your focus is writing, exercising, or simply dedicating time to mindfulness, make it a non-negotiable appointment with yourself.

To make this work, schedule your *One Thing* at a time when you're least likely to be interrupted. Block off time in your calendar, set reminders, and protect that time fiercely. It might mean waking up earlier, saying no to other commitments, or asking for support from those around you. Whatever it takes, prioritize your *One Thing* like the foundation it is.

2. **Simplify Your Environment**

Your environment has a profound impact on your ability to focus. A cluttered, distracting space makes it harder to stay committed to your *One Thing*. By intentionally shaping your environment to support your goals, you eliminate barriers and make it easier to stay on track.

When I began focusing on my health, I realized my environment wasn't setting me up for success. My pantry was full of temptations, and my kitchen wasn't conducive to meal preparation. To align my environment with my *One Thing*, I made intentional changes: I stocked up on high-protein snacks, prepped meals in advance, and removed the foods that didn't serve my goals. These small adjustments created a space where the path to honoring my commitment felt clear and straightforward.

Think about your own environment. If your *One Thing* is writing, set up a dedicated space that inspires creativity—free from distractions, with everything you need within reach. If your focus is on improving your fitness, organize your workout gear so it's ready to go. Simplify your surroundings to remove friction and make it as easy as possible to show up for your priority.

Remember, an environment that supports your *One Thing* isn't just about physical spaces—it's also about eliminating mental distractions. Turn off notifications, set boundaries with your time, and give yourself the mental space to fully engage with your focus.

3. **Align Your Day Around Your Focus**

The most successful days are designed with intention. To fully embrace your *One Thing*, let it guide the structure of your day. This doesn't mean neglecting other responsibilities—it means prioritizing your focus during your most productive hours and allowing other tasks to fall into place around it.

For me, aligning my day around my health meant starting each morning with small wins. As I mentioned previously, I began my day with a high-protein breakfast, prepped meals before work, and made movement part of my daily rhythm. Over time, those small actions snowballed into larger habits, like weightlifting, walking 10,000 steps a day, and even creating the discipline needed to launch a podcast and write this book.

Your *One Thing* deserves your best energy. Identify when you're naturally most focused and productive—whether that's first thing in the morning, during a midday break, or in the evening—and dedicate that time to your priority. By anchoring your day to your *One Thing*, you'll create momentum that carries through everything else you do.

It's also important to communicate your priorities to those around you. Let family, colleagues, or friends know about your commitment, so they can support you in protecting that time. Alignment doesn't mean ignoring other responsibilities—it means honoring your priorities in a way that supports your overall balance.

4. **Be Patient with the Process**

The process is rarely linear, and it certainly doesn't happen overnight. Making your *One Thing* a lifestyle requires patience, grace, and an understanding that progress takes time.

When I first started focusing on my health, I didn't see immediate results. Prioritizing protein didn't instantly make me feel stronger or more energized. But over time, that single action became the foundation for profound changes. It wasn't just about what I ate— it was about the mindset I was building. That patience paid off, as those small, consistent efforts, eventually, led to a lifestyle that supported the woman I wanted to become.

The same is true for you. Showing up for your *One Thing* every day—even when it feels insignificant—is what creates lasting transformation. Trust that the effort you're putting in now is laying the groundwork for the life you're building. Be kind to yourself on the hard days. There will be times when life feels overwhelming or when progress seems slow. Instead of giving in to frustration, remind yourself why you started. Reconnect with your vision, and trust that every small action is moving you closer to your goals.

Making your *One Thing* a lifestyle isn't about perfection—it's about consistency. By treating it as a non-negotiable, simplifying your environment, aligning your day around your focus, and being patient with the process, you're creating a foundation for lasting change. This isn't just a practice; it's a mindset shift that empowers you to take control of your journey and become the woman you've always envisioned.

Staying Aligned with Your Vision

Integrating your *One Thing* into your life is a powerful step toward transformation, but staying aligned with your bigger vision is just as important. As you grow and evolve, it's natural for your priorities to shift. What serves you today may not serve you tomorrow, and that's a good thing—it's a sign that you're making progress and moving closer to becoming the woman you envision.

To stay aligned, reflection is key. Regularly take time to evaluate whether your *One Thing* is still moving you forward. Ask yourself:

- Is this habit or action still helping me become the woman I want to be?

- Does this focus align with my values and aspirations?

- Have I outgrown this *One Thing*, and is it time to focus on something new?

These questions aren't about second-guessing your commitment but ensuring that your focus remains meaningful and impactful. Sometimes, your *One Thing* will evolve naturally as you grow. As I've talked about before, my health journey began with something as small as prioritizing protein at every meal. Over time, that single focus expanded into weightlifting, walking, and building a disciplined mindset that enabled me to tackle new challenges, like launching a podcast and writing this book. Staying aligned also means celebrating your progress. Each time you honor your commitment to your *One Thing*, you're not just moving closer to your goals—you're reinforcing your identity as someone who follows through. These small wins are proof of your transformation.

As you continue on this journey, give yourself permission to adjust your focus when needed, celebrate your growth at every stage, and trust that your *One Thing* will always lead you closer to the woman you're meant to be. Transformation is not just about what you achieve but about staying connected to your vision and honoring the incredible progress you're making along the way.

So, take a moment to reflect: What is the *one thing* that, by doing it, will make everything else easier or unnecessary? What habit or action will help you move closer to the woman you want to become? When you find your answer, commit to it fully. Trust that focusing on your *One Thing* will create the momentum you need to transform your life—just like it did for me. And remember: It's not about perfection. It's about progress, one small, powerful step at a time.

Grab your journal and reflect on these questions:

- What is the one thing I can focus on right now that will make everything else easier or unnecessary?

- Am I currently spreading myself too thin by focusing on too many priorities at once?

- Does my current environment support my One Thing, or are there distractions I need to eliminate to stay aligned with my focus?

- How can I measure whether my One Thing is still serving me and aligned with my vision as I grow and evolve?

- How will staying committed to my One Thing help me become the woman I want to be, even on the hard days?

Access the free workbook by scanning the QR code:

https://www.amandacahill.com/redefiningyouresources

Key Takeaways on the 'One Thing' Philosophy

- **Simplify to Amplify**: Transformation doesn't come from doing everything—it comes from doing the one action that matters most. Focusing on a single priority creates clarity, reduces overwhelm, and builds momentum.

- **Small Habits, Big Changes**: Consistently acting on one impactful habit—like prioritizing protein at every meal—can trigger a ripple effect of positive change in multiple areas of life, reshaping your identity and confidence over time.

- **Success Is Sequential**: Progress isn't simultaneous; it's a series of steps. Focus on the "first domino" that will set off a chain reaction, making subsequent actions easier or unnecessary.

- **Clarity Fuels Progress**: When you identify your One Thing, decision-making becomes simpler. Saying no to distractions and yes to your priorities helps you stay aligned with your vision.

- **Multitasking Is a Myth**: Concentrating on a single priority is far more effective than dividing your attention across many tasks. Focus brings flow and maximizes your productivity.

- **Align With Your Vision**: Your One Thing should reflect your values and help you move closer to the woman you want to become. Authentic alignment makes the habit easier to sustain and more meaningful.

- **Consistency Builds Confidence**: Treat your One Thing as a non-negotiable commitment. Every time you follow through, you reinforce self-trust and build the belief that you're capable of creating meaningful change.

- **Adapt as You Grow**: Your One Thing may evolve as you progress. Regularly reflect on whether it's still aligned with your vision and adjust your focus to stay connected to what matters most.

- **Transformation Is a Lifestyle**: Making your One Thing a part of your daily rhythm isn't about adding more—it's about aligning your life with your goals and values, creating sustainable change over time.

SECTION 4:
PROGRESS OVER PERFECTION

CHAPTER 12

Progress Not Perfection

"Small disciplines repeated with consistency everyday
lead to great achievements gained slowly over time."
– John C. Maxwell

In our pursuit of growth and transformation, it's easy to fall into the trap of perfectionism. We set high expectations for ourselves, striving to achieve flawless results, and feeling discouraged by even the smallest setbacks. But true progress isn't about perfection; it's about celebrating small wins along the way and recognizing that each step forward is a victory. This chapter explores the power of progress over perfection, encouraging you to embrace the journey and honor every achievement, no matter how small.

For a long time, I was my own harshest critic, constantly striving for perfect results. If I made a mistake or fell short of my expectations, I would feel frustrated and defeated, as though all my efforts were in vain. That mindset nearly stopped me from starting one of the most impactful endeavors of my life: my podcast.

When I first thought about launching a podcast, the idea felt daunting. I knew I wanted to create a space where I could connect with other women, share stories of growth, and encourage them to redefine their lives. But the moment I started thinking about the logistics—what the cover art would look like, how to record episodes, what equipment I needed, how to edit audio—I felt paralyzed. I didn't have it all figured out, and the fear of failing or creating something imperfect loomed large.

I told myself, *If I don't get this perfect from the start, it'll flop.* I convinced myself that everything had to be polished and flawless before I could even begin. I worried about how people might judge it or how I'd feel if it didn't meet my expectations. Perfectionism had me stuck, holding me back from even trying. But deep down, I knew that waiting for perfection wasn't an option. I had a message I wanted to share, and I couldn't let the fear of imperfection keep me from taking the first step. So, I decided to start messy. I recorded my first episode with a basic setup and no experience. I told myself it didn't have to be perfect—it just had to exist.

What happened next surprised me. The podcast didn't just survive—it thrived. Over time, I refined my process, got better equipment, and learned how to improve the quality of each episode. But even in those early days, the impact was immediate. I began receiving messages from listeners sharing how much the episodes resonated with them. They told me how they had shared the podcast with loved ones, how it had sparked conversations, and how it had encouraged them to take small steps in their own lives.

Today, that podcast has reached over 50 countries and continues to gain traction. It's a testament to the power of starting before you're ready and embracing progress over perfection. If I had waited for everything to be perfect, I would still be waiting. Instead, I took imperfect action, and it led to something greater than I could have imagined.

This is the lesson I want to share with you: Progress is always more powerful than perfection. Every small step you take, even if it feels imperfect, moves you closer to your vision. Each effort compounds over time, creating momentum and opening doors you never expected. Perfectionism may tell you to wait until you're fully prepared, but progress reminds you that the only way to get better is to begin.

Perfectionism is a heavy weight to carry. It tricks you into thinking that anything less than flawless isn't worth pursuing. But here's the truth: perfection is an illusion, and it's often the enemy of growth. Progress, on the other hand, invites you to try, to learn, and to grow. It encourages you to celebrate the messy middle, embrace imperfection, and trust that you're exactly where you need to be.

As we move through this chapter, we'll dive deeper into how perfectionism holds us back, how to embrace progress as a mindset, and how to reframe setbacks as valuable lessons. But for now, I want you to remember this: You don't have to have it all figured out to start. You just need to take one small step, and then another, and another. Transformation doesn't come from waiting—it comes from moving forward, one imperfect step at a time. And when you do, you'll look back and realize just how far you've come.

Redefine Progress: Celebrate the Journey, Not Just the Outcome

In a world that often glorifies the end result, it's easy to overlook the significance of the small steps that get you there. Progress, however, is not just about reaching a goal—it's about the growth, lessons, and resilience you build along the way. Redefining progress means shifting your focus from perfection and outcomes to honoring the consistent effort you put in, no matter how small.

Imagine climbing a mountain. Each step forward, no matter how slow or steady, brings you closer to the summit. If you only focus on reaching the top, you might miss the beauty of the journey—the views, the strength you're gaining, and the determination it takes to keep moving upward. Progress isn't linear, and it's not always visible in the moment. But each step you take lays the foundation for the transformation you're working toward.

When I started my podcast, I thought success would be measured by the number of downloads or glowing reviews. But early on, I realized that waiting for big milestones to validate my effort made the process feel overwhelming. Instead, I began celebrating the small wins: recording the first episode, receiving a heartfelt message from a listener, and showing up consistently even when it felt hard. Those moments of progress weren't just markers along the way—they were the journey itself.

Redefining progress also means giving yourself grace during setbacks. Life isn't perfect, and neither is transformation. There will be days when you stumble or feel like you're standing still. Instead of seeing those moments as failures, try to view them as opportunities to reassess and adjust. Progress isn't about avoiding mistakes; it's about learning from them and continuing forward with more clarity and intention.

A pivotal part of embracing progress is celebrating your wins, no matter how small. Did you show up for your *One Thing* today? Did you make a choice that aligns with your vision, even if it felt inconvenient? Those moments deserve recognition because they reinforce your identity as someone who follows through. When you acknowledge your progress, you build confidence and create momentum to keep going.

Redefining progress also changes the way you measure success. It's not about a perfect outcome—it's about the transformation happening inside you. Are you more consistent? More self-aware? More aligned with the woman you're becoming? These intangible markers are just as valuable as tangible achievements.

As you continue your journey, remind yourself: progress is personal. It doesn't need to match anyone else's timeline or standards. The small, steady steps you take today are what create the extraordinary transformation you'll see tomorrow. Celebrate them, embrace the imperfections, and trust that you're exactly where you need to be. Progress isn't just about getting closer to the summit—it's about finding joy, pride, and purpose in the climb.

Ditch the All-Or-Nothing Mentality

The all-or-nothing mentality is one of the biggest obstacles to progress. It convinces us that if we can't do something perfectly, it's not worth doing at all. This mindset keeps us stuck, afraid to try, and quick to give up when things don't go as planned. But transformation doesn't come from perfection—it comes from consistency. And consistency thrives when we embrace imperfect progress.

Think about a time when you set a big goal for yourself, like starting a new fitness routine. Perhaps you missed a workout or indulged in something off your meal plan, and suddenly it felt like the whole effort wasn't worth it anymore. You told yourself, *If I can't do this perfectly, why bother at all?* That's the all-or-nothing trap at work, whispering that one misstep invalidates all your hard work.

The reality is, perfection is an illusion. Life is messy and unpredictable, and waiting for perfect conditions or perfect performance will only delay your progress. Ditching the all-or-nothing mentality means recognizing that every effort counts, no matter how small or imperfect. It's about understanding that a stumble doesn't erase the steps you've already taken—it's simply part of the process.

When I launched my podcast, I had to confront my own all-or-nothing mindset. I thought every episode needed to be flawlessly planned, scripted, and executed before I could share it with the world. That belief kept me in a cycle of overthinking and procrastination. But, eventually, I realized that waiting for perfection was holding me back. I decided to release my first episode, knowing it wasn't perfect, but trusting that progress mattered more than flawlessness. That decision to let go of perfection didn't just help me move forward—it taught me that even an imperfect step can create momentum.

Ditching the all-or-nothing mentality also requires reframing what success looks like. Success isn't about doing everything right all the time; it's about doing something. If you miss a day of exercise, it doesn't mean you've failed your health journey—it means you can pick it up again tomorrow. If you're working on building a new habit and slip up, it doesn't mean the habit is broken. Each time you recommit to your goals, you're proving to yourself that progress is possible, even in the face of imperfection.

To overcome the all-or-nothing mindset, focus on showing up, even in small ways. If you can't fit in a full workout, take a 10-minute walk. If you're too tired to cook a full meal, make a simple choice that aligns with your goals. The key is to let go of the idea that every effort has to be monumental. Small, consistent actions add up, and they matter more than striving for perfection.

Lastly, remind yourself that progress isn't linear. There will be ups and downs, detours, and plateaus. But every time you choose to show up, even imperfectly, you're building resilience and momentum. You're proving to yourself that transformation isn't about all or nothing—it's about doing what you can with what you have and where you are.

As you redefine your journey, remember: imperfect action is still action. And action is what creates change. Let go of the pressure to do it all perfectly, and embrace the freedom that comes with showing up, doing your best, and knowing that every small effort is a step toward the woman you're becoming.

Build Resilience Through Self-Compassion

Resilience is often associated with toughness—the ability to push through challenges and never give up. But true resilience isn't about being unshakable or immune to setbacks. It's about adapting, growing, and continuing forward, even when the journey feels difficult. And one of the most powerful tools for building resilience is self-compassion.

Self-compassion doesn't mean lowering your standards or letting yourself off the hook. It means treating yourself with the same kindness and understanding you would offer a close friend. It's about recognizing that mistakes, setbacks, and missteps are part of the process—not signs of failure. In fact, research shows that people who practice self-compassion are more likely to bounce back from setbacks and stay committed to their goals, precisely because they don't waste energy beating themselves up.

When I started my podcast, self-compassion became a lifeline. There were moments when I felt overwhelmed by self-doubt, worrying that I wasn't prepared enough or that my episodes wouldn't resonate with anyone. In those moments, the harsh critic in my head was quick to chime in: *Who do you think you are to start this?* But instead of letting those thoughts derail me, I chose to meet them with compassion. I reminded myself that it was okay to feel uncertain—that it didn't mean I wasn't capable. I gave myself permission to be a beginner, to learn as I went, and to grow from the experience. That choice to extend grace to myself made all the difference.

Self-compassion is also crucial when we face setbacks. Let's say you're working toward a new habit, like exercising regularly, and you miss a week because life gets busy. The all-or-nothing mindset might tell you to give up entirely, while a self-critical voice might insist you've failed. But self-compassion offers a different perspective. It allows you to acknowledge the setback without judgment, reflect on what caused it, and recommit to your goals without carrying the weight of shame. Instead of seeing the missed week as evidence of failure, you see it as an opportunity to start fresh.

Building resilience through self-compassion also means recognizing the value of rest and recovery. Transformation isn't just about action—it's also about balance. If you're constantly pushing yourself without pause, burnout becomes inevitable. Self-compassion helps you honor your limits, giving yourself permission to rest when needed without feeling guilty. It's a reminder that rest isn't a sign of weakness—it's a vital part of staying strong for the long haul.

To practice self-compassion, start by shifting your inner dialogue. Pay attention to how you speak to yourself when things don't go as planned. Would you speak to a friend that way? If not, replace those critical thoughts with words of encouragement and understanding. For example, instead of saying, *I can't believe I messed this up again,* try saying, *It's okay—I'm learning and growing, and this doesn't define me.*

Another powerful way to cultivate self-compassion is to celebrate your small wins, even when progress feels slow. Each step you take, no matter how small, is evidence of your effort and commitment. By acknowledging and honoring those wins, you're reinforcing the belief that you're capable of growth and transformation.

Finally, self-compassion helps you embrace imperfection as part of the journey. It teaches you that you don't have to have everything figured out to make progress. It reminds you that setbacks don't mean you're failing—they mean you're human. And when you approach yourself with grace and understanding, you build the resilience needed to navigate the ups and downs of redefining your life.

As you continue on your path of transformation, remember that self-compassion isn't a sign of weakness—it's a source of strength. It's what allows you to get back up when you stumble, to keep going when the road feels uncertain, and to believe in your ability to create the life you envision. By treating yourself with kindness, you're not only building resilience—you're creating a foundation of self-trust, courage, and unwavering commitment to becoming the woman you're meant to be.

Step Into Your Power: Redefining Failure and Success

One of the most transformative shifts you can make on your journey is redefining what failure and success mean to you. So often, we see failure as the ultimate setback—a roadblock that confirms our worst fears about ourselves. Meanwhile, we equate success with perfection, believing it must look a certain way or meet specific external standards. But what if we chose to step into our power by reimagining these concepts? What if failure wasn't an end but a beginning, and success wasn't about meeting someone else's expectations but about living in alignment with our vision and values?

Redefining failure starts with reframing it as feedback. Instead of seeing failure as a judgment of your abilities or worth, view it as a lesson—a stepping stone on the path to growth. When I started my podcast, I had no guarantees it would succeed. I worried that if it didn't gain traction or resonate with listeners, it would be a sign that I wasn't cut out for it. But over time, I realized that even if something didn't go as planned, it didn't mean I had failed. Each episode, even the ones that didn't land as well as I'd hoped, taught me something valuable: how to improve my content, connect with my audience, and refine my message.

Failure isn't about falling short—it's about what you choose to do next. When you redefine failure as an opportunity for growth, you take back the power it once held over you. Instead of being paralyzed by the fear of making mistakes, you're free to take bold, meaningful action. You're no longer afraid to try because you know that every experience—success or setback—is part of your transformation.

Redefining success is just as crucial. So often, we measure success by external metrics: a promotion, a certain number on the scale, or praise from others. While there's nothing wrong with celebrating these achievements, true success goes deeper. It's about living in alignment with your values, honoring your commitments, and becoming the woman you want to be. It's about progress, not perfection—about showing up each day with intention and courage, regardless of the outcome.

Take the podcast as an example. When I started, my initial measure of success was simple: to create something meaningful and share my voice. But as the podcast grew—reaching over 50 countries and impacting lives in ways I never imagined—I realized that success wasn't just about numbers or reach. It was about the courage it took to begin, the discipline to keep going, and the joy of knowing I was making a difference. Success wasn't defined by how "perfect" each episode was; it was defined by the impact it had on others and the growth it sparked within me.

When you step into your power, you take ownership of how you define success and failure. You're no longer bound by societal expectations or the fear of judgment. Instead, you're guided by your own vision and values. You recognize that failure is part of the journey—a necessary ingredient in growth—and that success is about living authentically and purposefully. This shift doesn't just free you from fear—it empowers you to dream bigger. When failure no longer feels like something to avoid at all costs, you're willing to take risks, try new things, and push past your comfort zone. And when success is measured by how aligned you are with your vision, you can find joy and fulfillment in the process, not just the outcome.

To redefine failure and success, start by asking yourself some key questions: What have I learned from my past failures? How have those lessons shaped who I am today? What does success look like for me—not according to others, but according to my own values and goals? The answers to these questions will help you reframe your perspective, giving you the clarity and confidence to move forward with purpose.

As you continue on your journey of redefining yourself, remember that stepping into your power isn't about avoiding failure or chasing an unattainable version of success. It's about embracing the messy, imperfect process of growth. It's about taking bold, intentional action, knowing that each step—no matter how small—brings you closer to the life you want to create. By redefining failure and success, you're giving yourself permission to own your story, celebrate your progress, and trust in your ability to create a future that reflects the woman you're becoming.

The Ripple Effect of Progress

Progress, no matter how small, has a unique ability to create a ripple effect that extends far beyond the initial action. Each step you take, each habit you build, and each choice you make sets off a chain reaction of positive change, shaping not just your present but also your future. This is the magic of the compounding effect—a concept we explored earlier that illustrates how small, consistent actions accumulate over time to create exponential results.

Let's revisit why this idea is so transformative. Imagine you're stacking dominoes. Tipping over the first domino might feel insignificant—it's just one, after all. But that small motion carries enough energy to topple the next domino, and the next, until the entire row falls. This sequence isn't about the size of the first domino; it's about the power of momentum. Progress works in the same way. Each small win creates energy and motivation that propels you toward the next step, amplifying your impact with each action.

When I started my podcast, I didn't set out with the goal of reaching over 50 countries or impacting thousands of listeners. My focus was simple: produce the first episode. That single action felt daunting at the time, but once I pressed record and released the episode, something shifted. Completing that first step gave me the confidence to move forward, and before I knew it, I was planning the next episode, and then the one after that. Over time, those seemingly small steps compounded into a platform that has touched lives around the world. The ripple effect of that progress still amazes me.

This is the essence of compounding: The more you show up and honor your commitments, the greater the momentum you build. Even actions that feel small or insignificant in the moment can lead to life-changing transformations. For instance, consider how committing to 10 minutes of daily journaling might spark insights that lead to a clearer vision for your future. That clarity could inspire a new habit, like waking up earlier to work on a passion project, which might eventually grow into a business or a creative endeavor that transforms your life. The impact of one small action can ripple outward in ways you can't yet imagine.

What makes the ripple effect so powerful is its ability to extend beyond you. When you commit to your growth, the progress you make inspires those around you. Maybe your habit of prioritizing your health motivates a friend to start their own wellness journey. Perhaps your commitment to pursuing your goals shows your children what's possible when you believe in yourself. Progress, when shared or witnessed, creates ripples that touch lives far beyond your own.

This interconnected nature of progress is what makes it such a vital part of redefining yourself. By focusing on small, intentional actions, you're not just creating change for yourself—you're contributing to a broader wave of positivity and possibility. Each step you take reinforces the belief that transformation is possible, both for you and for those who look to you for inspiration.

The compounding effect also serves as a reminder to trust the process, even when results feel slow or imperceptible. Change doesn't happen overnight. It's easy to feel discouraged when you don't see immediate results, but remember: Progress often works beneath the surface, building momentum in ways you may not recognize until later. Just as a tree takes time to grow roots before it bears fruit, your small actions are laying the foundation for something extraordinary.

So, how can you harness the ripple effect of progress in your life? Start by committing to one small, impactful action. Choose something that aligns with your vision and feels manageable. Then, show up for it consistently, even when it feels insignificant. Each time you honor that commitment, remind yourself that you're creating ripples that will, eventually, lead to waves of transformation.

Ask yourself: *What is one small step I can take today that will move me closer to the woman I want to become? How might that step influence other areas of my life? How can I celebrate the progress I've made so far, no matter how small?*

By focusing on the ripple effect of progress, you'll not only create momentum for your own growth but also inspire others to embrace their own journeys. Progress isn't about perfection or grand gestures—it's about showing up, day after day, and trusting that each small step matters. When you harness the power of compounding, you're building a foundation for transformation that is both sustainable and impactful. You're not just taking steps forward—you're creating ripples of change that will shape the woman you're becoming and the world around you.

Progress as a Journey, Not a Destination

Embracing progress over perfection requires a shift in mindset and a willingness to see growth as a journey rather than a destination. It's about honoring each step, celebrating each win, and giving yourself grace in moments of struggle. Progress isn't linear; it's a winding path filled with twists, turns, and moments of reflection. By focusing on the journey rather than the outcome, you're cultivating resilience, self-compassion, and a deep sense of purpose.

The path to transformation isn't about achieving a perfect result; it's about becoming the person you aspire to be, one small win at a time. As you continue on this journey, remember that each step, no matter how small, is a testament to your growth. Each win is a reminder of your strength, and each moment of progress brings you closer to the woman you're meant to become.

Embrace the power of progress, knowing that transformation is built through small, consistent actions. Celebrate each step, honor your journey, and trust that every small win is bringing you closer to the life you envision. Progress, not perfection, is the key to lasting change and a life of purpose, resilience, and fulfillment.

Grab your journal and reflect on these questions:

- Where in my life am I holding back because of perfectionism?

- What does success mean to me personally, beyond external validation or societal expectations?

- How do I define failure?

- How can I shift my mindset to celebrate progress rather than focus solely on outcomes?

Access the free workbook by scanning the QR code:

https://www.amandacahill.com/redefiningyouresources

Key Takeaways on Progress, Not Perfection

- **Progress Over Perfection**: True growth isn't about achieving flawless results but about taking consistent, imperfect steps forward. Each small win brings you closer to your vision.

- **Perfectionism Is a Trap**: The pursuit of perfection can paralyze you and delay meaningful action. Let go of the need for everything to be flawless and focus on starting where you are.

- **Celebrate Small Wins**: Acknowledging and celebrating small achievements helps build momentum and reinforces your commitment to your goals. These wins are the foundation of transformation.

- **Redefine Progress**: Shift your focus from the end result to the journey. Every step forward, no matter how small, contributes to your growth and resilience.

- **Ditch the All-Or-Nothing Mentality**: Let go of the idea that you must do everything perfectly or not at all. Even small, imperfect actions create meaningful change over time.

- **Build Resilience Through Self-Compassion**: Treat yourself with kindness when setbacks occur. Self-compassion helps you recover quickly and recommit to your journey without shame or self-criticism.

- **Redefine Failure and Success**: View failure as feedback and success as alignment with your values and vision. This mindset empowers you to take bold action without fear of judgment.

- **Harness the Ripple Effect**: Small, consistent actions compound over time, creating a ripple effect of positive change in your life and inspiring others around you.

- **Progress Is a Journey, Not a Destination**: Embrace the winding path of growth, celebrating each step and trusting that you're exactly where you need to be.

CHAPTER 13

Reflect and Refine

"Your life does not get better by chance, it gets better by change—and intentional reflection fuels that change." – Jim Rohn

Growth is not a straight line. The woman you are today is not the same as the woman you were a year ago—and she won't be the same as the woman you'll be a year from now. That's the beauty of transformation: it's dynamic, fluid, and deeply personal. As you progress on your journey, there will come a time when you need to pause, take stock, and adjust. Your goals, habits, and vision must evolve to align with the woman you are becoming. Nothing changes if nothing changes.

I learned this lesson firsthand when I reached a milestone that once felt like the pinnacle of my career: stepping into an exciting executive-level role at a new company. It was everything I had envisioned for years— greater responsibility, opportunities to lead, and the chance to create a real impact in my industry. It felt like the culmination of all my hard work, the fulfillment of a vision I had been pursuing with intentionality and discipline.

But once the initial excitement subsided, I found myself facing an unexpected question: What now? For so long, my focus had been crystal clear. I had set habits and goals that supported my vision of becoming an influential leader. I networked tirelessly, worked on my leadership skills, and consistently showed up as someone who added value. These habits had become second nature, and they worked. They got me to where I wanted to be. Yet, standing at this new threshold, I realized something profound: The habits and strategies that got me here weren't necessarily the ones that would carry me forward. I had achieved a massive goal, but in doing so, I had outgrown the vision that had guided me for so long. It was time to reflect and refine.

This is the nature of growth—it doesn't end when you achieve a milestone. In fact, reaching a goal often marks the beginning of a new chapter. What got you to one point in your life isn't guaranteed to get you to the next. The same habits that helped you climb one mountain might not serve you as you prepare to climb another. Recognizing this isn't a failure—it's a sign of evolution.

I knew I needed to step back and reassess. What did I want this new role to mean for me? How did I want to grow within it? What kind of leader did I want to be? And perhaps most importantly, how did this new role fit into the bigger picture of the woman I was becoming? These questions required deep reflection, and answering them meant letting go of the idea that I needed to have it all figured out.

Reflection is often the part of the journey we resist the most. When we achieve a goal, there's a temptation to keep pushing forward without pausing to assess what's next. But ignoring this step can leave you feeling stagnant, even after reaching a milestone. You might find yourself going through the motions, relying on habits that no longer align with your vision. That's why taking the time to reflect isn't just helpful—it's essential.

For me, this process began with acknowledging that my vision had to change. The vision that guided me to this new role had served its purpose, but now I needed a new one. My priorities had shifted, and I needed to define what success looked like in this new phase of my career and life. This wasn't an easy process—it required me to get honest with myself about what I wanted and to accept that I didn't have all the answers right away.

Once I started to articulate my new vision, I realized that my goals and habits also needed to evolve. The habits that helped me secure this role—like networking and sharpening my skills—were still valuable, but they weren't enough on their own. Now, I needed to focus on habits that would help me excel in my new position and grow into the leader I aspired to be. This meant prioritizing new skills, like delegating effectively, fostering a collaborative team culture, and balancing the demands of leadership with my personal well-being. This process of refinement wasn't about discarding everything that had worked before—it was about building on it. I asked myself: *What habits and goals still serve me? Which ones need to be adjusted? And what new actions will help me move toward my next vision?*

The answers weren't always clear, and the process wasn't linear. There were moments of doubt and trial and error. But through reflection and refinement, I began to feel a renewed sense of alignment. I was no longer operating on autopilot or relying on outdated strategies. Instead, I was moving forward with intention, crafting a life that reflected the woman I was becoming—not just the woman I had been.

This experience taught me a valuable lesson: Growth is an ongoing process of recalibration. It's not about setting goals once and following them blindly; it's about staying connected to your vision and being willing to adapt as you evolve. Reflection allows you to take stock of where you are, while refinement ensures that your actions remain aligned with where you're going.

The same will be true for you. As you progress on your journey, there will come moments when you need to pause and ask yourself: *Is the path I'm on still leading me to the life I want? Are my goals and habits aligned with the woman I'm becoming?* These moments aren't setbacks—they're opportunities to grow with intention.

Redefining your goals and habits as you evolve is a powerful act of self-leadership. It's a reminder that you are the architect of your life, capable of adjusting your course whenever needed. As you move into this next chapter, embrace the dynamic nature of growth. Celebrate how far you've come, reflect on where you want to go, and refine your actions to align with your ever-evolving vision. This is how you continue to redefine yourself—by honoring the woman you are today while staying committed to the woman you're becoming.

When to Refine

Refinement is not about abandoning your goals the moment things feel tough—it's about making thoughtful adjustments to ensure your actions and intentions remain in harmony with the person you are becoming. It's recognizing that growth is not static, and neither is your vision. Refinement allows you to evolve with purpose, staying aligned with your goals as life shifts around you. But how do you know when it's time to refine? Let's explore the moments when reflection and recalibration become essential.

1. **When Your Vision Shifts**

    One of the clearest signals that it's time to refine is when your vision begins to evolve. Life isn't static—neither are your priorities, passions, or the circumstances shaping your journey. What once felt like your ultimate goal may no longer resonate as you grow and gain clarity about what truly matters.

    When I started my podcast, my vision was focused on creating a space where I could share my story and connect with other women. It was simple and meaningful at the time, but as the podcast grew, I realized my vision had shifted. It was no longer just about sharing my voice—it was about creating a global community, a platform that could inspire women in over 50 countries. That expansion of vision required me to refine my approach. I had to rethink how I structured episodes, how I engaged with my audience, and even how I measured success.

The same will happen in your journey. You might start with a goal to improve your health, only to realize later that it's about more than physical fitness—it's about cultivating energy and resilience to show up fully in every aspect of your life. Or perhaps you begin a new career path with a focus on building skills, only to discover a deeper passion for leadership or mentoring others. When your vision shifts, it's not a sign of failure—it's a sign of growth. Refining your goals and habits to align with this new vision ensures that you're staying true to the woman you're becoming.

2. **When Progress Stalls**

Have you ever felt like you're doing everything "right" but still not making the progress you expected? It's frustrating, disheartening, and often a clear sign that it's time to refine. Stalled progress doesn't mean your goals are unattainable—it might mean that your current strategies or habits need adjustment.

When progress stalls, it's an invitation to step back and reassess. Are your goals still realistic for this season of life? Are your habits creating the impact you hoped for, or are they just keeping you busy? Sometimes, stalled progress can be a result of outgrown habits—actions that once pushed you forward but no longer challenge or inspire you.

For example, if you've been working toward a fitness goal by walking every day, there might come a time when your body and mind need a new challenge. Refining your approach could mean adding strength training or trying a new form of movement to reignite your excitement and results. The same applies to personal growth or career aspirations—if the tools or strategies you've been using no longer move the needle, it's time to refine your approach.

3. **When You're Ready for the Next Level**

As you progress, the goals and habits that once felt challenging will eventually become second nature. When you find yourself in this space—when what once stretched you now feels comfortable—it's time to refine and reach for the next level.

Think of this as leveling up. The woman you are today has the capacity to take on challenges that might have seemed overwhelming a year ago. Refining your goals doesn't mean disregarding what you've already accomplished—it means building on that foundation to unlock your next phase of growth.

When I transitioned into my executive role, I quickly realized that the habits that had helped me secure the position weren't enough to help me excel in it. Networking and skill-building had been crucial in my journey to that point, but now I needed to develop new habits, like delegating effectively and leading with vision. Refinement allowed me to focus on the areas where I could grow further, ensuring that I wasn't just maintaining the status quo but continually stepping into my potential.

For you, refining for the next level might mean reassessing what "success" looks like in this phase of your journey. It could mean challenging yourself to take on a leadership role, deepen a personal relationship, or tackle a new skill that aligns with your evolving vision.

Refinement is a powerful tool for staying connected to your purpose and ensuring that your efforts are always meaningful and impactful. It's not about giving up on your goals—it's about evolving with them. Each time you refine, you're reaffirming your commitment to growth and transformation.

So, ask yourself: *Has my vision shifted? Am I feeling stuck or unmotivated? Have I outgrown the habits that once served me?* These questions will guide you to the moments where refinement is needed most. By embracing this process, you're not just adjusting your goals and habits—you're aligning your life with the woman you're becoming, ensuring that every step forward is intentional, empowered, and deeply personal.

How to Reflect and Refine

The process of reflection and refinement is where true transformation takes root. It's not about abandoning what you've built—it's about realigning with the woman you're becoming and ensuring that your efforts are working for you, not against you. Refinement is your chance to pause, take stock, and adjust your course to stay connected to your vision. Let's walk through this powerful process step by step.

1. **Revisit Your Vision**

   Start by reconnecting with your long-term vision. Ask yourself: *Who is the woman I'm becoming? What does she prioritize? What does her life look and feel like?* These questions act as your compass, guiding you toward goals and habits that truly matter.

   Think of your vision as the North Star. It's not set in stone—it evolves as you do—but it always offers direction. As life changes, your priorities may shift, and that's okay. Revisit your vision regularly to ensure it still resonates with your values and aspirations.

   For example, when I stepped into my new executive role, I realized that my previous vision—focused on career advancement—needed to evolve. I had reached a significant milestone, but I couldn't stop there. My new vision became about leading with impact, nurturing my team, and finding a balance between professional success and personal fulfillment. Reflecting on this shift allowed me to adjust my focus and ensure that my habits supported this new chapter.

Take time to journal, meditate, or have a conversation with someone you trust about your vision. Clarity here is essential; it will anchor you as you refine your goals and habits.

2. Set a Reflection Routine

Reflection is most powerful when it's consistent. By creating a regular routine for reflection, you ensure that you're actively assessing your progress and recalibrating your efforts, rather than letting life's demands take over.

Here's how to structure a reflection routine:

- Weekly Check-Ins: At the end of each week, set aside 10–15 minutes to review your progress. What went well? What challenges arose? What adjustments could you make moving forward?

- Monthly Reviews: Dive deeper into how your habits and goals align with your vision. Are you making progress, or do certain areas feel stagnant? Use this time to celebrate wins and identify opportunities for growth.

- Quarterly Overviews: Reflect on the bigger picture. Is your vision still resonating with you? Are your goals stretching you in meaningful ways? This is your chance to recalibrate and set intentions for the next phase of growth.

Building a reflection routine doesn't have to be time-consuming. Even a few moments of intentional thought can provide clarity and momentum. By making reflection a habit, you'll stay connected to your growth and aligned with your evolving priorities.

3. **Evaluate Your Habits**

Habits are the building blocks of your daily life, but not all habits remain effective over time. As you grow, some habits may lose their relevance or need fine-tuning to align with your evolving goals. Reflect on the habits you've built so far:

- Are they creating the results you want?

- Do they still feel meaningful and aligned with your vision?

- Are they challenging you in a way that promotes growth?

For instance, if you've been journaling every morning but find it has become routine without much impact, it might be time to refine that habit. Perhaps you add a specific focus, like gratitude, or use prompts to explore deeper insights. Similarly, if your exercise routine feels stagnant, you might consider introducing new activities to reignite your enthusiasm and keep your body challenged.

Reflection isn't about criticizing your habits—it's about being honest with yourself. What's working? What isn't? What could be adjusted to better serve your goals? By evaluating your habits, you're taking the first step toward meaningful refinement.

4. **Identify Areas for Growth**

Growth thrives when you intentionally seek out opportunities to stretch yourself. Identifying areas where you feel stuck, uninspired, or under-challenged can help you focus your energy on meaningful change.

To pinpoint these areas, reflect on your current habits and goals:

- *What areas of my life feel stagnant or unfulfilling?*

- *What skills or habits could I develop to move closer to my vision?*

- *Where am I avoiding growth due to fear or discomfort?*

For instance, stepping into my executive role revealed areas for growth I hadn't prioritized before, like developing stronger delegation skills and fostering team collaboration. Recognizing these gaps allowed me to set new goals and create habits that supported my evolution as a leader. By proactively identifying areas for growth, you're taking charge of your journey and ensuring that your transformation remains intentional and forward-moving.

5. Adjust with Intention

Refinement doesn't mean starting from scratch. It means taking what's already working and making it even better or letting go of what no longer serves you to create space for what will. Adjusting with intention requires small, thoughtful tweaks that align with your growth.

For example, when I stepped into my executive role, I realized that the habits that got me there—like networking and skill-building—needed to evolve. My new priorities included strategic decision-making and team leadership, so I adjusted my focus accordingly. Instead of spending time on broad networking events, I began cultivating deeper connections with key stakeholders and mentoring team members. These shifts weren't drastic, but they made a profound difference in how I showed up in my role.

Adjustments can be as simple as increasing the intensity of your workouts, dedicating focused time to a new skill, or shifting from broad goals to more specific actions. The key is to ensure that every adjustment moves you closer to your vision.

6. **Set New Benchmarks**

Refinement is an opportunity to set fresh goals that reflect your growth. These benchmarks should stretch you without overwhelming you, offering a balance between challenge and achievability.

For example, if your initial goal was to drink more water daily, and you've mastered that habit, your next benchmark might be creating a balanced meal plan to support your energy and focus. If you've been exercising three times a week, your new goal could involve training for a 5K or incorporating strength training to build endurance.

When setting benchmarks, ask yourself:

- *What's the next level for me?*

- *What small steps can I take today to move closer to that level?*

- *How will I measure progress and celebrate wins along the way?*

Setting new benchmarks ensures that your growth remains dynamic and forward-moving. It keeps you from becoming stagnant and reinforces the belief that you're capable of achieving more.

7. **Celebrate Evolution**

Finally, take time to celebrate how far you've come. Reflection isn't just about identifying areas for improvement—it's about acknowledging your progress and honoring the work you've done to get here.

When I transitioned into my new role, I often found myself focused on the next challenge, forgetting to appreciate the milestones I had already achieved. It wasn't until I paused to reflect on the journey—

remembering the moments of uncertainty, the risks I took, and the habits I built along the way—that I realized how much I had evolved. Those moments of celebration fueled my motivation and reminded me of my resilience.

Celebrating evolution isn't just about big achievements—it's about recognizing the small wins that mark your growth. Maybe you've consistently shown up for your One Thing, or perhaps you've embraced progress over perfection in a way that feels freeing. These are moments worth celebrating because they reflect the transformation happening within you.

Reflection and refinement are ongoing practices that keep you aligned with your vision and grounded in your purpose. By revisiting your vision, evaluating your habits, adjusting with intention, setting new benchmarks, and celebrating your evolution, you're creating a roadmap for continuous growth.

Remember, this process isn't about perfection—it's about progress. It's about honoring where you've been, embracing where you are, and confidently stepping into where you're going. Transformation is not a one-time event; it's a journey of reflection, refinement, and renewal. Trust the process and trust yourself. You have everything you need to evolve into the woman you're becoming.

The Importance of Staying Aligned

As you grow, staying aligned with your vision becomes even more important. Alignment means that your goals, actions, and habits reflect the woman you want to become. It's about choosing paths that resonate with your values and creating a life that feels true to who you are. Reflection and refinement are tools that help you stay aligned, ensuring that each step you take is purposeful and intentional.

When you stay aligned, you're building a life that feels authentic and fulfilling. You're not just pursuing goals for the sake of achievement; you're creating a life that reflects your deepest desires and aspirations. This alignment brings a sense of peace, purpose, and confidence, allowing you to move forward with clarity and joy.

Growth as a Continuous Journey

Reflection and refinement remind us that growth is a continuous journey. There's no final destination, no moment when we've "arrived." Instead, transformation is a process of evolution, a series of steps that bring us closer to our true selves. Embracing this journey means honoring both the highs and lows, the moments of clarity and the times of uncertainty.

As you move forward, remember that each reflection, each refinement, is a step toward greater alignment. Each adjustment brings you closer to a life that feels purposeful, fulfilling, and true. Transformation isn't about reaching a specific endpoint; it's about creating a life that resonates with your values, aspirations, and unique journey.

Allow yourself to grow and evolve with grace, knowing that the path to transformation is paved with reflection, flexibility, and resilience. Embrace each stage of the journey, and trust that every choice, every adjustment, is bringing you closer to the woman you're becoming.

Grab your journal and reflect on these questions:

- What aspects of my current vision still resonate with the woman I am becoming, and what might need to evolve?

- Are there any habits or strategies I've outgrown that no longer serve my current season of life?

- When was the last time I paused to celebrate how far I've come?

- What areas of my life feel stagnant, and how could refining my approach help me create new momentum?

- What is one specific habit or goal I could adjust today to better align with my vision?

- How will I create space for regular reflection to ensure my actions and habits stay aligned with my vision?

Access the free workbook by scanning the QR code:

https://www.amandacahill.com/redefiningyouresources

Key Takeaways on Adjusting Goals and Habits as You Evolve

- **Growth Is Dynamic**: The woman you are today is not the same as the woman you'll be in the future. Your goals, habits, and vision must evolve to reflect the person you're becoming.

- **Milestones Are New Beginnings**: Achieving a goal is not the end—it's the start of a new chapter. The habits that got you here may not take you to your next level, requiring reflection and refinement.

- **Reflection Is Essential**: Regularly pause to assess whether your goals and habits align with your evolving vision. Avoid the temptation to keep pushing forward without recalibrating your path.

- **Refinement Is Growth**: Adjusting your habits and goals is not failure—it's an acknowledgment of evolution. It allows you to honor where you are while staying connected to where you want to go.

- **Recognize When to Refine**:
  - When your vision shifts: As your priorities and values evolve, ensure your goals reflect the life you're building.
  - When progress stalls: Adjust strategies or habits that no longer serve you to reignite momentum.
  - When you're ready for the next level: Build on your current successes by stretching into new challenges.

- **Set a Reflection Routine**:
  - Weekly check-ins to assess progress and challenges.

o Monthly reviews to evaluate alignment with your vision.

o Quarterly overviews to recalibrate and set intentions.

- **Evaluate and Adjust Habits**: Identify which habits still serve you, which need refinement, and which new habits will support your next phase of growth.

- **Set New Benchmarks**: As you grow, establish fresh goals that stretch you and align with your current vision. Progress happens when you challenge yourself meaningfully.

- **Celebrate Your Evolution**: Honor the milestones and small wins along the way. Recognize how far you've come and use that momentum to fuel future growth.

- **Stay Aligned**: Ensure your actions, goals, and habits reflect your values and aspirations. Alignment brings authenticity, purpose, and fulfillment.

- **Growth Is a Journey**: Transformation isn't about reaching an endpoint—it's an ongoing process of reflection, refinement, and renewal. Trust the journey and honor your evolution.

CHAPTER 14

Step Into Your Power

"There is no force more powerful than a woman determined to rise." – W.E.B. Dubois

As you turn these final pages, take a moment to reflect on how far you've come. This book was never about giving you a roadmap to a predetermined destination—it was about helping you find your own path. You've explored the foundations of confidence, crafted a vision that inspires you, cultivated goals and habits that support your growth, and embraced the power of progress over perfection. Every chapter has been a step forward, guiding you to this pivotal moment: stepping into your power and fully becoming the woman you've envisioned.

Stepping into your power isn't a single moment or milestone—it's a way of living. It's choosing to show up every day as the truest, most aligned version of yourself, even when the road is uncertain. It's about embracing the woman you are while continuing to evolve into the woman you're becoming. This journey has been about discovering not just what you want, but who you are, and now it's time to claim that with intention and confidence.

When I reflect on my own journey, I think about the culmination of years of effort that led me to step into my executive-level role at a new company. As I've shared before, it was everything I had envisioned— greater responsibility, opportunities to lead, and the chance to create real impact. For years, I had set goals and built habits to prepare for this moment. But as the initial excitement subsided, a profound realization set in: reaching this milestone wasn't the end. In fact, it was the beginning of a new chapter that required me to step into my power in ways I hadn't anticipated.

Suddenly, I found myself asking, *What now?* The habits and strategies that had helped me secure this role weren't necessarily the ones that would help me thrive in it. My vision had to evolve, and with it, my goals and approach. At first, this realization felt overwhelming—was I ready for this next level? Could I rise to the challenges ahead? But as I reflected, I understood something powerful: stepping into your power isn't about having all the answers. It's about trusting yourself enough to take the next step, even when the path forward feels uncertain.

The same is true for you. Along this journey, you've built confidence and resilience. You've learned to trust yourself, embrace growth, and let go of perfection. These qualities are your foundation as you move into the next phase of your life. Stepping into your power means carrying forward everything you've learned while staying open to the possibilities that lie ahead. It's about integrating your vision, habits, and mindset into a life that reflects who you are and who you're becoming.

This isn't about waiting for the perfect moment to begin—it's about recognizing that you're ready now. Not because everything is perfect, but because you've decided it's time. You've already proven that you can grow, adapt, and thrive, even in the face of challenges. Each choice you've made to prioritize your growth has prepared you for this moment.

As you reflect on your journey, take pride in how far you've come. Think about the woman you were when you started and the fears or doubts that might have held her back. Then, consider the woman you are today—how she has grown, what she has overcome, and the strengths she has uncovered. Stepping into your power isn't about becoming someone entirely new; it's about embracing who you are while continuing to evolve.

This moment is an invitation. It's a chance to own your story, to live in alignment with your vision, and to choose a path that feels authentic and meaningful to you. It's about trusting yourself to navigate whatever comes next, knowing that you already have everything you need to succeed. The journey doesn't end here—it continues, and with each step, you'll grow stronger and more aligned with the woman you've always envisioned.

Take a deep breath, and step forward with intention. This is your life, your moment, and your opportunity to claim the power that has always been within you. The woman you've been working toward isn't a distant idea—she's here, in you, ready to emerge. Trust her, believe in her, and let her lead you toward the life you've envisioned. You've got this.

The Power of Self-Belief

Believing in yourself is the cornerstone of empowerment. It's the quiet, unshakable foundation that allows you to step into your power, take risks, and pursue the life you've envisioned. Without self-belief, even the clearest vision or the most well-thought-out plan can falter under the weight of doubt. But with it? You become unstoppable—not because the road is always easy, but because you trust your ability to navigate it, no matter what lies ahead.

Self-belief isn't about being confident every single day. It's not about feeling fearless or certain at every moment. Instead, it's about trusting yourself, even on days when doubt creeps in. It's about being your own number-one cheerleader, the voice that reminds you of your worth and your potential when the world—or your own mind—tries to convince you otherwise.

When I stepped into my new executive role, the excitement of achieving this milestone was quickly followed by moments of uncertainty. Questions swirled in my mind: *Am I really ready for this? What if I don't meet expectations? What if I fail?* These doubts felt heavy, threatening to overshadow the sense of accomplishment I had worked so hard to achieve. But in those moments, I reminded myself of one simple truth: I didn't get here by accident. I got here because I showed up for myself, again and again, even when it was hard. I trusted myself enough to take the steps that led me to this moment, and I could trust myself to take the next steps, too.

That's the essence of self-belief—it's not about having all the answers. It's about trusting your ability to figure them out. It's about recognizing that you've overcome challenges before and that you have the resilience, resourcefulness, and courage to do it again. It's about grounding yourself in your own worth, knowing that you are enough, exactly as you are, to take the next step forward.

Self-belief is especially important on the days when doubt arises because those are the days when it's hardest to move forward. It's easy to trust yourself when everything is going well, when the path feels clear, and when progress is visible. But when setbacks arise or when the road ahead feels uncertain, that's when self-belief becomes your anchor. It's the voice that says, "Even if I don't have this all figured out, I trust myself to keep going."

One of the most powerful ways to strengthen your self-belief is to become your own advocate. Celebrate your wins—big and small—and remind yourself of the progress you've made. Too often, we focus on what we haven't done or where we've fallen short, forgetting to acknowledge how far we've come. But every small victory, every step forward, is evidence of your capability. Let those moments be fuel for your belief in yourself.

Equally important is learning to quiet the inner critic that tries to undermine your confidence. That voice might tell you you're not ready, that you're not good enough, or that you're bound to fail. But you don't have to listen to it. Instead, counter those thoughts with affirmations of your worth and your ability, just as we've talked about over the course of this book. Remind yourself of the challenges you've faced and overcome. The fact that you're here, reading these words, and committing to your growth is proof of your strength.

Self-belief also grows through action. Every time you show up for yourself—whether it's honoring a commitment, taking a step toward your vision, or simply choosing progress over perfection—you reinforce your trust in your ability to succeed. Confidence doesn't come from waiting until you feel ready; it comes from doing, from taking imperfect action and proving to yourself that you're capable.

Let me be clear: Believing in yourself doesn't mean ignoring your doubts or pretending you're fearless. It means acknowledging those feelings and choosing to move forward anyway. It's about saying, "I may not know exactly how this will unfold, but I trust myself to handle it." That's the power of self-belief—it allows you to embrace uncertainty with courage and grace.

As you step into your power, remember that self-belief is a practice, not a destination. There will be days when it feels easier and days when it feels harder, but every time you choose to trust yourself, you're strengthening that foundation. You're proving to yourself that you are enough, that you are capable, and that you are worthy of the life you're creating.

Being your own cheerleader doesn't mean you won't need support from others—it means recognizing that your belief in yourself is the foundation upon which all other support is built. It's about knowing that while encouragement from friends, family, or mentors is valuable, the most important voice in your life is your own. When you choose to lift yourself up, cheer yourself on, and trust in your ability to grow, you unlock a power that no external validation can replicate.

So, take a moment to reflect on everything you've accomplished so far. Think about the challenges you've faced, the goals you've achieved, and the growth you've experienced. Let those moments remind you of your strength and your resilience. And when doubt arises, let it be an invitation to reconnect with your self-belief—not to question it.

Stepping into your power means embracing the fullness of who you are, including the parts of you that still feel uncertain. It's about standing tall in your worth, trusting your ability to navigate whatever comes next, and believing in the woman you're becoming. You are your greatest ally, your strongest advocate, and your most reliable source of support. Believe in yourself, because you are more than capable of creating the life you envision—and you've already proven that to yourself time and time again.

Take Ownership of Your Journey

One of the most transformative realizations you can have is this: **You are the architect of your life.** Every step you've taken, every choice you've made to build confidence, set a vision, cultivate habits, and embrace imperfection has been leading you to this moment. Owning your journey isn't about having all the answers or achieving perfection—it's about recognizing the power you hold to create a life that reflects your deepest values and aspirations.

Owning your journey means rejecting the notion that life simply happens to you. It's about stepping out of the passenger seat and taking control of the wheel. This shift in mindset is profound because it places the responsibility—and the opportunity—squarely in your hands. Life isn't a series of random events; it's a canvas you're painting with every decision you make. And while you can't always control the circumstances, you can always control how you respond to them.

To truly own your story is to stop outsourcing your worth to external validation, achievements, or opinions. It's about embracing the belief that your value isn't tied to what others think of you or what you've checked off a list. Your worth is inherent—it exists because you exist. From that place of self-worth, you can take full ownership of your life.

Owning your story means viewing every experience—both the triumphs and the setbacks—as an integral part of your growth. Challenges aren't roadblocks; they're opportunities to build resilience and discover strength you didn't know you had. Mistakes aren't failures; they're lessons that guide you closer to the woman you're becoming. When you embrace this perspective, life stops feeling like something that's happening to you and starts feeling like something that's happening for you.

Take a moment to reflect on your journey so far. Think about the times you doubted yourself but showed up anyway. Consider the moments when things didn't go as planned, yet you found a way forward. Those experiences weren't just hurdles—they were stepping stones, teaching you the value of perseverance and self-trust. They were shaping you into the strong, capable woman you are today.

Owning your journey is also about reclaiming your power. For too long, you might have given away that power—to societal expectations, to fear, or even to the voices of self-doubt. But stepping into ownership means taking it back. It's acknowledging that while you can't control everything, you always have the power to choose how you respond, how you grow, and how you move forward.

Reclaiming your power doesn't mean ignoring the influence of external forces—it means choosing to prioritize your voice above all others. It's about trusting your intuition and honoring your desires, even when they don't align with what others expect of you. It's about recognizing that you're the author of your story, and you get to decide how each chapter unfolds.

Owning your journey requires courage. It means taking responsibility for your choices, your growth, and your happiness. It's easier to blame circumstances or wait for someone else to make the first move, but real empowerment comes from taking accountability for your life.

When you take ownership, you're no longer waiting for the perfect moment, the perfect plan, or the perfect conditions. You understand that progress begins when you take the first step. Ownership is what turns your vision into action and your action into transformation. It's what allows you to move forward even when you're uncertain, knowing that you're capable of navigating whatever comes your way.

A critical part of owning your journey is celebrating the choices you've made along the way. Too often, we focus on what we could have done better or where we fell short, overlooking the courage it took to make a choice in the first place. Every decision you've made—big or small—has shaped the path you're on. Even the moments that didn't go as planned have taught you valuable lessons and led you closer to your truth.

Think about the choice to pick up this book and commit to your growth. That was an act of ownership. Think about the times you honored your habits, chose progress over perfection, or took a risk despite fear. Those moments are worth celebrating because they reflect your willingness to take charge of your life. Owning your journey is about recognizing the power in those choices and letting them fuel your confidence as you move forward.

Owning your journey doesn't mean having everything figured out. It means trusting yourself to navigate change as it comes. Life is dynamic, and so are you. Your vision, goals, and habits will evolve as you grow, and that's a good thing—it's a sign of progress. Ownership means giving yourself permission to adjust your course without questioning your worth or your ability.

This process of refinement, which we explored in the previous chapter, is a key part of ownership. It's about regularly checking in with yourself, ensuring that your actions align with your vision and values. It's about being honest with yourself when something isn't working and having the courage to make a change. Ownership isn't about perfection—it's about alignment.

To fully embrace ownership, you must shift your mindset from one of limitation to one of possibility. Instead of focusing on what's holding you back, focus on what's within your control. Instead of dwelling on past mistakes, focus on the lessons they've taught you. Instead of fearing the unknown, focus on the opportunities it holds.

When you own your journey, you step into a life of empowerment. You stop waiting for permission, validation, or guarantees, and you start creating the life you want. You recognize that you have everything you need within you to succeed because you've already proven it to yourself.

You are the architect of your life. Every choice, every action, and every moment of self-belief is building the foundation for the woman you're becoming. Take pride in your journey, trust in your power, and embrace the truth that you are capable of creating a life that reflects your vision, your values, and your unique story. This is your life—and you have everything you need to own it fully.

The Ripple Effect of Your Power

Your journey to stepping into your power isn't just about transforming your own life—it's about the undeniable ripple effect your growth has on those around you. When you align with your vision, embrace your authenticity, and show up as the woman you've envisioned, your transformation becomes an invitation for others to do the same. Your courage and confidence light the way, inspiring others to believe in their own potential.

I've seen this ripple effect firsthand through my podcast. When I first hit "record," I didn't imagine the impact it would have on others. At the time, I was simply stepping into my power, sharing my story, and creating a space for women to feel seen and heard. But what started as a personal endeavor quickly grew into something bigger. Listeners began reaching out, sharing how an episode resonated with them, how it sparked a meaningful conversation with a loved one, or how it encouraged them to take a small step toward their own goals. The stories they shared weren't just about the impact of the podcast—they were about the transformations those ripples created in their own lives.

This is the magic of the ripple effect. By stepping into your power, you give others permission to do the same. You show them what's possible when they align with their true selves and take bold steps forward.

How Your Transformation Inspires Others

The ripple effect starts with something small—a single action, decision, or mindset shift. Perhaps you choose to focus on your health and begin prioritizing movement in your daily life. Your increased energy, positivity, and confidence naturally influence those around you. Your partner might be inspired to join you on walks. Your children might start mimicking your healthy habits. Your friends might notice your glow and ask what you've been doing differently. Without even realizing it, your commitment to growth becomes a catalyst for others to explore their own potential.

And this isn't limited to grand, public endeavors like starting a podcast or writing a book. The ripple effect is just as powerful in the small, personal ways you show up. When you prioritize alignment and create positive changes in your life, the people closest to you—your family, your friends, your colleagues—can't help but notice. Your presence, energy, and example become an unspoken encouragement for them to reflect on their own lives.

The Ripple Effect on Family

One of the most profound places the ripple effect shows up is within your family. When you start living in alignment, it changes how you show up at home. Your energy shifts. You have more patience, more joy, and more space to be fully present. These changes may feel subtle at first, but they create a foundation of positivity and possibility that your loved ones can't help but feel.

Think about this: When your children see you setting and achieving goals, they learn the value of persistence and discipline. When they watch you embrace imperfection and celebrate progress, they learn that it's okay to try and fail. They see that growth is a journey, not a destination. Your actions become a powerful lesson in what it means to live authentically and courageously.

Even if you don't have children, the ripple effect can still transform your household. A partner might feel encouraged to pursue a dream they've been putting off, inspired by your willingness to step into the unknown. Friends might begin to think differently about their own potential, seeing what's possible through your example. The changes you make in your own life create waves of possibility for those you care about most.

Your Ripple Effect Is Your Legacy

The beauty of the ripple effect is that it extends far beyond what you can see. The encouragement you give someone today might inspire them to make a change tomorrow. That change might lead to a conversation with someone else, creating a ripple you never even realize you started.

This is your legacy: the impact of your growth, courage, and commitment to living authentically. It's not about how many lives you touch directly—it's about the chain reaction you set into motion simply by being true to yourself.

I still receive messages from podcast listeners who tell me how an episode changed their perspective or gave them the nudge they needed to take action. These stories remind me that the ripple effect isn't just about the big, visible moments. It's about the small, quiet shifts that happen when someone feels seen, heard, and inspired by what you've shared.

The Ripple Effect in Your Life

So, what does this mean for you? It means that every step you take toward living in alignment matters—not just for you but for everyone around you. Whether you're pursuing a dream, cultivating a new habit, or simply showing up as your authentic self, you're creating ripples of inspiration.

Imagine the impact your transformation could have on your family, friends, colleagues, or community. Imagine how your courage to step into your power might inspire someone else to take the first step on their own journey. Imagine the ripple effect of you becoming the woman you've envisioned—not just for your life, but for the world around you.

Your ripple effect doesn't have to be loud or grand—it just has to be real. When you show up with authenticity, alignment, and purpose, you're creating a legacy that extends far beyond what you can see. And that legacy, built on your growth and empowerment, is something no one can take away.

As you continue on this journey, remember: Every step you take creates ripples. Every action, no matter how small, has the power to inspire. Your transformation isn't just about you—it's about the impact you're creating in the lives of everyone you touch. So keep going. Keep growing. The ripples you create today will shape a brighter, more empowered tomorrow—for you and for those around you.

An Empowering Final Exercise

As we reach the culmination of this journey, it's time to anchor your transformation with one final, empowering exercise: writing a letter to the woman you've become. This isn't just an activity—it's a moment of profound reflection and celebration, a chance to connect deeply with your growth and set intentions for the chapters yet to come. Let this letter be a testament to your journey and a declaration of your continued evolution.

Step 1: Begin with Gratitude

Start your letter by expressing gratitude to yourself. Imagine speaking to the woman who has overcome challenges, made bold choices, and shown up with courage and determination. Thank her for her resilience, for her willingness to grow, and for her commitment to becoming the best version of herself.

For example:

> "Dear [Your Name],
>
> Thank you for everything. Thank you for showing up on the hard days, for pushing through the fear of imperfection, and for believing in yourself even when doubt crept in. You've worked so hard to become the woman you are today, and I'm so proud of the choices you've made and the strength you've found."

Let this moment of gratitude remind you of how far you've come and all the steps that brought you here.

Step 2: Celebrate Your Growth

Reflect on the journey you've taken. Highlight the milestones, both big and small, and celebrate the habits, mindset shifts, and decisions that have shaped your transformation. This is your moment to honor the work you've done and the resilience you've built.

Think back to the moments when you felt uncertain but chose to act anyway. Recall the times when you embraced progress over perfection, learned from setbacks, and stayed true to your vision.

For instance:

> "You've grown so much. Remember when you didn't think you could follow through on your goals? Look at you now. You've built confidence through action, cultivated habits that align with your vision, and proven to yourself time and time again that you're capable of incredible things. Every step you've taken, no matter how small, has been a step toward the life you're living today."

Let your words celebrate not just the destination but the path that brought you here.

Step 3: Envision the Next Chapter

Now, turn your focus to the future. Write about the woman you're still becoming. Picture her vividly: What does she prioritize? What does her life look and feel like? What dreams is she chasing?

Use this part of the letter to articulate your vision for the next phase of your journey. Set intentions that feel aligned with your deepest values and aspirations.

For example:

> "I see her—the woman you're becoming. She's bold, compassionate, and fearless in her pursuit of purpose. She

continues to grow and evolve, embracing challenges as opportunities for growth. She's making an impact, inspiring others, and showing up for herself in ways she never thought possible. Her dreams are big, but her belief in herself is even bigger."

This is your opportunity to connect with the limitless potential of who you're becoming.

Step 4: Seal It with Affirmation

Close your letter with a powerful affirmation of your journey and your future. Commit to revisiting this letter whenever you need encouragement, clarity, or a reminder of your strength.

You might end with something like:

"You are powerful beyond measure. You are worthy of every dream you've dared to chase. Keep believing in yourself, keep moving forward, and trust that every step you take is bringing you closer to the woman you are meant to be. The best is yet to come."

Keep It Close

Once you've written your letter, place it somewhere special. Save it in a journal, tuck it into a keepsake box, or create a digital copy that's easily accessible. This letter is more than words on a page—it's a declaration of your power, a celebration of your progress, and a guiding light for the road ahead.

By writing this letter, you're acknowledging all that you've accomplished and paving the way for the future you're creating. It's a practice in self-belief, self-compassion, and self-empowerment—a final act that ties together everything you've learned on this journey.

You've shown yourself what's possible. Now, write your story with intention, courage, and unwavering belief in the woman you're becoming. The pen is in your hand—make it count.

Your Journey Is Just Beginning

Stepping into your power doesn't signify the end of the road—it marks the beginning of something extraordinary. This book was never about an ending; it was about equipping you to embark on the limitless journey of becoming. You've built the foundation, cultivated habits that empower you, and embraced a vision that inspires your every step. You've proven to yourself that you are capable of extraordinary transformation, and now, the path ahead is yours to design.

Take a moment to honor the woman you've become. She is resilient. She is courageous. She has faced doubt, fear, and uncertainty, and she has chosen to rise anyway. Remember, stepping into your power isn't about never feeling doubt or fear—it's about knowing, deep in your soul, that you can navigate those feelings and still move forward. It's about trusting yourself and embracing every stage of the journey, knowing you have the tools to shape your life in alignment with your vision.

As you move forward, know that your power lies not just in your accomplishments but in your unwavering commitment to growth. There will be more challenges, more moments of uncertainty, and even setbacks—but there will also be more triumphs, more lessons, and more opportunities to step into the fullness of who you are. Trust that every step you take, no matter how small, is a step toward the woman you're becoming.

You are the author of your story. You are the architect of your dreams. And the life you envision isn't just possible—it's already within reach. Every time you choose to honor your values, prioritize your vision, and embrace progress over perfection, you are stepping into your power.

The world is waiting for the unique magic only you can bring. You are more capable, resilient, and worthy than you may yet fully realize. So, step forward with confidence, curiosity, and boldness. The woman you've envisioned is already within you—she's been there all along, waiting for you to believe in her. This is your moment. Claim it unapologetically. Embrace the journey with an open heart and know that every step is part of your beautiful evolution. The best is yet to come, and it's yours for the taking. Now, go redefine the world as only you can. The world needs the power of your light—let it shine brightly.

Grab your journal and reflect on these questions:

- What does stepping into my power mean to me?

- How can I use the tools I've cultivated to shape the next chapter of my life?

- What legacy do I want to leave through the ripple effect of my growth?

- How will I continue to believe in myself, especially during moments of doubt and uncertainty?

- What can I do today to honor my journey and take a bold step forward?

Access the free workbook by scanning the QR code:

https://www.amandacahill.com/redefiningyouresources

Recap of the Letter-Writing Exercise:

Write a letter to your future self:

- **Step 1: Begin with Gratitude.** Thank yourself for your resilience, courage, and the steps you've taken to get where you are today.

- **Step 2: Celebrate Your Growth.** Highlight the milestones and mindset shifts that have shaped your journey.

- **Step 3: Envision the Next Chapter.** Paint a vivid picture of the woman you're becoming—her priorities, dreams, and impact.

- **Step 4: Seal It with Affirmation.** Close with a declaration of belief in your ability to continue growing and evolving.

Keep your letter close as a source of encouragement and clarity whenever you need it. It's a tangible reminder of your power, progress, and unwavering potential.

Key Takeaways on Stepping Into Your Power to Become the Woman You Envisioned

- **Stepping Into Your Power Is a Journey, Not a Destination**: It's about showing up daily as your truest self and continuing to evolve into the woman you've envisioned. Your journey is dynamic and ongoing, not a singular moment or milestone.

- **Self-Belief Is Your Foundation**: Trust in your ability to navigate challenges, even when doubt creeps in. Confidence grows through action—each small step reinforces your belief in yourself.

- **The Power of Imperfect Action**: You don't need to have everything figured out to move forward. Progress begins when you choose to act, knowing that growth and clarity come through doing, not waiting.

- **Own Your Journey**: Take responsibility for your choices, growth, and happiness. Recognize that life doesn't just happen to you—you are the architect, capable of creating a life that aligns with your vision and values.

- **Your Ripple Effect Inspires Others**: By stepping into your power, you inspire those around you to do the same. Your growth creates ripples of positivity and possibility that extend far beyond your immediate reach.

- **Celebrate Your Evolution**: Acknowledge how far you've come, the challenges you've overcome, and the strength you've built. Each step, no matter how small, is a testament to your resilience and growth.

- **The Power of Vision and Alignment**: Stay connected to your vision and let it guide your actions. Regularly reassess your goals and habits to ensure they align with the woman you're becoming.

- **Transformation Is Continuous**: Growth doesn't end—it's a lifelong process of reflection, refinement, and renewal. Each chapter builds on the last, bringing you closer to a life that reflects your deepest values and aspirations.

Acknowledgement

Writing *Redefining You* has been one of the most rewarding and transformative experiences of my life, but I didn't walk this path alone. This book is a reflection of the incredible support, love, and encouragement I've received along the way, and I am endlessly grateful to the people who made it possible.

To my husband Chris: Your unwavering belief in me, especially on the days when I doubted myself, means more than words could ever express. Thank you for being my anchor, my biggest cheerleader, and the one who always reminds me of my strength. Your love and support made this journey possible, and I couldn't have done it without you.

To my son Camden: You are my greatest inspiration and the reason I strive to be the best version of myself every single day. Thank you for reminding me of what truly matters in life and for filling my days with love and joy.

To my family and close friends: Thank you for your endless encouragement, patience, and understanding. You've listened to my ideas, cheered me on, and supported me through every high and low of this process. Your faith in me has been a constant source of strength.

To my readers: This book is for you. Thank you for trusting me to be part of your journey. I hope these words empower you to step into the best version of yourself, just as this process has done for me. I hope it's given you permission to dream bigger, trust yourself more, and step fully into the life you're meant to live.

Lastly, to every woman who has ever felt stuck, unseen, or unsure of how to move forward: Your strength, resilience, and courage inspire me. I hope this book serves as a reminder that you are not alone, and that you are capable of creating a life that feels truly, authentically yours.

With gratitude and love,
Amanda Cahill

URGENT PLEA!

What did you think of *Redefining You*?

As you turn the final pages of *Redefining You*, I just want to take a moment to say—**thank you.**

Thank you for investing in yourself, for showing up, and for allowing me to be a small part of your journey. Writing this book has been one of the most meaningful experiences of my life, and knowing that these words have reached you means more than I can express.

If *Redefining You* has resonated with you in any way, **it would mean the world to me if you left a review on Amazon**. Your review not only helps other women discover this book, but it also lets me know how this journey has impacted you.

I'd love to continue the conversation with you—connect with me on www.amandacahill.com and share your biggest takeaways!

Remember: You are capable. You are worthy. And your story is still being written.

About the Author

 Amanda Cahill is a Corporate Executive, Investor, Author, MBA graduate, and mom who soared up the corporate ladder in just a decade—proving that ambition and authenticity can go hand in hand. Although she seemed to have it all—thriving career, supportive relationships, and dynamic enthusiasm—Amanda discovered there was more to life than checking the traditional boxes of success. Embracing a path of self-development, she began questioning the status quo and realized that many women felt stuck, unfulfilled, and hungry for something greater.

Today, Amanda is on a mission to help ambitious women break free from the ordinary. Drawing on her own journey and the lessons she's learned along the way, she has mentored thousands to redefine their dreams, challenge old narratives, and create a life they're genuinely proud of. Her approach is equal parts strategy and heartfelt guidance—empowering women to make bold moves, forge meaningful connections, and rewrite their own definitions of success.

Connect with Amanda

Website: www.amandacahill.com

LinkedIn: www.linkedin.com/in/amanda-cahill

Instagram: www.instagram.com/amandacahill